Gift from Focus on
FPC Conference - March 22-23, 1995
Colorado Springs, CO

Walking the Tight Rope

Walking the Tight Rope

Balancing Family Life
& Professional Life

Dr. Tom Barrett

WALKING THE TIGHTROPE
© 1994 by Thomas J. Barrett, Ph.D.

Published by Business/Life Management, Inc.

Cover design by Multnomah Graphics
Illustration by Krieg Barrie

Printed in the United States of America.

Dr. Tom Barrett
Business/Life Management, Inc.
1980 Gallows Road
Suite 200
Vienna, Virginia 22182

All Scripture references are from the Revised Standard Version of the Bible, © 1946, 1952, 1971, 1973, Division of Christian Education, National Council of the Churches of Christ in the USA.

To Bill Secor

As a professor par excellence,
you fed my hunger for learning
while I was in graduate school.

As a psychologist,
you modeled how to bring wisdom,
skill, and compassion into your work with people.

As a mentor,
you gave me a love for life.

As an exhorter,
you gave me the drive to finish
my master's degree, pursue a Ph.D.,
and write this book.

In the process I have learned to call you my friend.

May I be to others what you have been to me.

Contents

Acknowledgments

Dr. R.H. "Swede" Anderson and Dr. Bill McKelvie . . . you saw the value of this book long before I did. There were many days when I found endurance via your vision.

Mark Petersburg, Walt Tomme, and Loren Bruce . . . your friendship and encouragement were invaluable during this project. You guys personify what it is to be a friend. Thanks for being in my corner.

Curtis Lundgren . . . without you as an agent/coach I would still be lost in the strange and mysterious world of book publishing.

Liz Heaney and Robin Georgioff . . . thanks for the excellence and skill you bring to your work as editors. This book is far better because of you.

Mike Petersen and Pat Edmonds at Multnomah Graphics . . . what a joy to work with you and your team. Your creativity, combined with your commitment to excellence, made you a pleasure to work with . . . thanks for your patience with this rookie.

Beth Price and Becky Gilman . . . I cannot recall how many times you bailed me out with computer assistance, editing, and printing of the early manuscript. Thanks for being there for me.

The ten Senate and Congressional wives who agreed to meet with me week after week to discuss each chapter as it was written . . . I never would have finished this task without you. Your endless patience and careful analysis of my research and writing for accuracy, fairness, and balance were invaluable. I am deeply indebted to you for caring about this book.

Most importantly, my wife, Linda, and my daughters, Lindsay and Stephanie . . . while I was researching and writing this book you were often the ones who had to "hold your breath" and run "the hidden marathon." What you did was not unnoticed by me. Thanks for making home such a refreshing place to return to at the end of a long day. My greatest honors in life are simply to be called your husband and your dad.
Everything else is a distant second.

Introduction

I stood with the congressman looking at the picture of his freshman class. His class has been in Congress for well over a decade. We talked about those in his class who have already died, been defeated, or retired. As we finished, he looked once more at the picture full of eager faces and said with a mixture of confusion and sadness, "And we were the class that was going to change the Congress and the world."

Many people come to Washington, D.C., with hopes of making an impact, bursting with the honor of playing in the big leagues. As the country's star players, they come with expectations of making an enormous difference. They are going to get the district, state, country, or world working properly. They are going to "straighten this place up."

But with time many realize that their presence has made no appreciable difference in Washington. Instead, they discover they are the ones who have changed. They did not change the place . . . but the place has changed them.

This transformation is often quiet and unexpected. In fact, the change has often occurred long before it is noticed. Like undetected termites systematically gnawing away at the substructure of a house, political life can erode the foundations of a person's private life. And this erosion is often unnoticed until the structural damage to the person's life and relationships is so severe that they are barely salvageable.

I wrote this book for a specific purpose: to help people in political life win in their private lives. This book is about helping people win where it matters most in the end . . . in their primary relationships. Far too many people win in their public and political lives, but fail in their private lives. And this, as one member told me with tears in his eyes, "is a very hollow victory."

For years I have watched members suffer the agony of submitting themselves to a thumbs up or down vote from their constituents. They know that if they lose sight of their constituents, they will eventually lose their seat in Congress. What some ignore is that the members of their family also have a vote. And this vote occurs much more often than every two or six years. In the end, rejection by a spouse is far more devastating than rejection by a state. And losing the affection or confidence of your child hurts much more deeply than losing a seat in Congress.

This book was written for members of Congress; it is not about them. It is offered simply as a means of insight. After spending over ten thousand hours with members of Congress in the last fifteen years, I have come to care deeply for them. This book will help members become more aware of what their family thinks, feels, and needs. It will also help members become more self aware.

Sadly, the Washington community rarely encourages people

in their personal lives and it refuses any responsibility for contributing to personal failure. When it comes to their private lives, men and women in Washington are completely on their own. That is why they need firm boundaries for determining their life styles and schedules. Without these, they can—and do—become the victims of their own success. The success of their public lives leads to the collapse of their private lives.

Washington political life can numb peoples' senses, obscure their values, and fill their schedules. It offers unlimited opportunities of interesting places to go, unusual things to do, and wonderful people to meet. For the politically elite, Washington provides a chance to meet just about everyone in the world. The one person many don't meet is themselves. They can lose sight of who they are and what is important.

I hope this book does several things for you. I hope it lessens your sense of aloneness in this isolated Washington culture. I also hope it will ask you hard questions and say some hard things.

People in the political world and those at the top of the corporate world frequently tell me they rarely have anyone who will shoot straight with them. As their stature or position increases, the number of people that will risk being candid with them decreases. Even their friends and colleagues grow more reluctant to be honest with them about their blind spots or weaknesses. Many end up surrounded by people who will tell them the things they want to hear, but almost no one tells them the things they need to hear. It allows them to grow older without growing up.

The children's story, *The Emperor's New Clothes*, is wonderfully pertinent for those in Washington political life. Think about it. When was the last time a trusted friend came to you and said, "You look ridiculous. Don't you know you are not wearing any clothes? Why are you strutting around like a peacock?" Who loves you enough to risk being truthful with you?

I am convinced many members—particularly those with the greatest maturity and psychological health—long for someone to be direct with them. They hunger for candid thinking on crucial issues in their lives.

The insights and illustrations on these pages were gleaned from scores of men and women in Congress who have allowed me to learn from them. This book is a tribute to their courage, candor, and wisdom. It reflects what they have taught me and asked me to write for their friends and colleagues. I am grateful for their encouragement, friendship, and permission to use their life stories. (All of the stories and illustrations used in this text are true and are used with the permission of the individual involved. But the name of the person has been changed in each instance to protect their anonymity.)

A few final thoughts before jumping into our first chapter.

This book will be useful for those of you who are not members of Congress. The issues addressed on the following pages are common to men and women in many working professions. Whether you are in the military, business, athletics, education— your struggle is similar to those of members of Congress. As you read this book, think about your own life.

The tone of this book will not seem balanced or politically correct to some readers. It is full of illustrations from the lives of men in Congress. Women made up less than 2 percent of the Senate and Houses when I first began working on Capitol Hill over fifteen years ago. While I am grateful for a Congress that has more women, I cannot represent myself as an expert on what it is like to be a woman in Congress. I hope that my writing does apply to female members of Congress—but as a researcher, I can't assume that it does. I've intentionally written this book to appeal more to men than to women. Additionally I have made an effort to write in a style that will hold the interest of men. I know how difficult it is to get some men to read a book that is not business or sports related.

I hope this book will be used as an instructional guide for incoming politicians and for those considering public life. It can help prevent people from being personally overwhelmed while learning to swim in political waters. If I can catch them before they get swept away, their work will be easier and mine will have been worthwhile.

Finally, I am aware of the strong negative feelings people have toward Washington as a collective whole. I am aware of the minimal trust and confidence they have toward Congress as a body. I know that many think members are overpaid and underworked. But I disagree. I have developed enormous respect for the vast majority of members of Congress. I have come to know them as individuals, as people—not as politicians. I care about them and their well being. They are my friends.

This book is written to help my friends win. Not in the game of politics, that is not my area of expertise. I want my friends to win at the game of life. For when all is said and done, this is the only game that counts.

CHAPTER 1

GET OUT OF THE SPOTLIGHT

"It is a luxury to be understood."
—Ralph Waldo Emerson

Capitol Hill. It is an extraordinary place: dynamic, fast, and full of prodigiously gifted people. These people are often exceptionally intelligent, highly verbal, and very opinionated. They are talkers, shakers, and movers. They are the opinion shapers and policy makers.

But many people on Capitol Hill lack one thing. They are not skilled listeners. And to be lacking as a listener can be fatal—especially in marriage.

If people in the political world want to have healthy and balanced relationships, they need to learn one thing: how to remove themselves from center stage. They need to "get out of the spotlight."

Remembering to do this can be difficult if you are in political life, particularly if you are a member of Congress. Wherever you go, you are often given center stage. For you, traffic is halted, pedestrians are stopped, elevators are held, and doors are opened. Over time it's easy to come to expect this lifestyle as normal. You become accustomed to hearing:

"Oh, please sit here at the head table."

"Come over here, I want you to meet someone."

"Would you mind saying a few words?"

"Would you mind if we took your picture?"

Such requests occur every day.

On numerous occasions I have accompanied a member to dinner with a group of people who are not members of Congress. When the group does not know that a member has joined them, this is what happens: Initially we are standing around or sitting down and eating. Everyone talks. Everyone is equal. People take turns being the center of attention. A natural give and take occurs in the discussion.

As soon as it becomes known that a person at the table is a member of Congress, everything shifts. Like E. F. Hutton, the member will speak and others will listen. All give and take is gone as the member dominates the conversation. One former member insightfully observed that at social gatherings where he was unknown, he was often patient and quiet. When he left Congress he was able to see that he had not really been patient in those moments—he knew that eventually someone would inevitably ask him, "What do you do?" From that moment on he would be given the spotlight for as long as he wanted it. He simply had to wait.

If members are not careful, they lose the ability to defer and give attention to someone else. It's as if the spotlight of attention has been focused on them for so long, that it has rusted in place and can no longer be moved and focused on someone else.

For members who have been exposed to the spotlight for a long time, life on Capitol Hill can be toxic. When the toxicity has reached a dangerously high level, careful observers often see the following changes in a member's behavior.

- A diminished ability to *listen,* especially to one's spouse or family.

- Difficulty focusing on other people for long periods of time. Often the visual acuity is so poor that the member cannot see beyond himself or herself.

- The member talks more without saying more. Often the conversation is limited to topics that pertain to the member. Others—again especially spouses and children—are not permitted to talk about their own interests and desires.

We All Want Our Moment in the Sun

No matter where you go, people are trying to grab the spotlight. They are hoping, waiting, or jockeying for their moment in the sun.

I often notice this when I counsel couples. It's as if there is a spotlight in the ceiling of my office. Both people are reaching for it so they can put it on themselves. They compete for it without even knowing it. They are not necessarily being selfish, they desperately want their spouse to know what their world and life are like. They want to be understood.

All of us have competed for the spotlight. Think about it. Have you ever been at an important business meeting and had something you really wanted to say? You waited and waited and finally the moment seemed right. You took a deep breath, collected your thoughts, and shared your very best ideas. All eyes were on you—but not for long.

What happened the moment you finished speaking? Someone else jumped in and grabbed the spotlight and your ideas or suggestions were swept away, lost, ignored. On the outside you acted like you didn't care. But inside you felt rejected or insignificant. If you had enough ego strength, you waited to take back the spotlight at the next opportunity. If not, a part of you quietly died along with your idea.

Most of us look for our chance to grab the spotlight rather than listening to the person who has it. I wonder what would happen if more of us were willing to share it. Recently I heard about an entire group of people who willingly gave the spotlight to a little boy named Tommy.

Tommy had Down's syndrome. He played on a baseball team but he never once hit the ball when it was his turn to bat. One day his big moment came. Tommy was at the plate and the pitcher threw the ball to him. He swung at the ball with all his might and for the first time ever he hit it. The ball dribbled out to the pitcher who threw him out long before he got to first base.

Tommy didn't notice. This was his moment, his day. He was so excited that he took off running. After reaching first base he headed for second. He rounded second and bolted for third. After clearing third he went full tilt for home plate. While heading for home, something extraordinary happened. All the fans in the bleachers were on their feet cheering Tommy on. As Tommy crossed home plate, both dugouts emptied as teammates and opponents alike surrounded him. They gathered around him to give him hugs, high-fives, and pats on the back.

It was Tommy's moment in the spotlight.

There is something magnificent in watching people learn to give the spotlight of attention, interest, and respect to others.

One Spotlight with Too Small a Beam

If you are to survive life in Washington, you must periodically inspect your spotlight. You might want to ask yourself, "How big is the beam of my spotlight?" To answer this question, picture an auditorium that is completely dark except for the beam of one spotlight shining down onto the stage. If this spotlight represented your ability to focus on others, how wide a beam would it have? Is it big enough to be shared by others? Can your family fit into it? Can the people who work for you, or with you, get into it? Or do you take the praise and credit for their ideas and labor?

Cathy painfully discovered the narrowness of the beam of her husband's spotlight. After a grueling campaign, her husband waited on election night with hundreds of people (what only Washingtonians could call their "closest friends"). Finally, enough votes had come in to ensure that he was the victor. He rose to make his acceptance speech. As the victory music was playing, all of the people were standing, applauding, and cheering. The member stood there enjoying "the thrill of victory." He waved and nodded to the crowd. He made all the right moves and said all the right things.

Except for one minor *faux pas*. In the excitement of the moment, he forgot to invite his family up onto the stage. An astute staff member discreetly advised him to invite his family to join him on stage. Some in the crowd never even noticed, but his family will never forget.

How big is your spotlight?

Greg is one of the most loyal, gifted, and dedicated people I have ever met in my years of working with people on the Hill. He worked for one of the "Old Bulls" of the Senate. His boss was one of the venerable and once towering figures of the Senate. His seat was safe and his place in Senate history was secure.

When the senator announced his retirement, Greg met with him and asked if he would consider endorsing Greg's run for a seat in the House. To the staffer's dismay, the senator felt threatened and became indignant. He accused the staffer of disloyalty and never fully trusted him again.

What had triggered such a selfish response? The senator had grown too accustomed to people investing their lives and energy in making him look good. He could not tolerate a person asking him to share his spotlight, even briefly. Gradually, he had lost the capacity to think of anyone else. He was stuck on center stage. Even when his career was winding down, he couldn't bear to have a person in his employ thinking about their life rather than his.

Like the Wizard of Oz, the man that had seemed larger than life was rather small when studied closely. He could have left a legacy in the life of a gifted, young politician. Instead, his legacy is buried in the annals of the Senate library and archives.

Are You Growing Weeds or Flowers?

If you want to keep a sharp eye on your capacity to share the spotlight, then you must resist assimilating a Washington myth.

Men and women all over the city erroneously accept this myth as truth. It goes like this:

*Who I am, and what I do, is so important that I am
exempt from the normal responsibilities of life.*

No one ever officially announces or teaches this myth, but it flourishes in the lives of many leaders until it blows up in their faces and they realize that their personal relationships are in trouble because of neglect. When this happens many people understand that a law of agriculture also applies to human relationships: *Uncultivated ground grows weeds not flowers.*

We may have many pressing and important responsibilities in our professional lives. Our jobs may be incredibly important. But they will never exempt us from the realities and obligations of our private lives. No matter how prestigious the position, no magical power exists that suddenly eliminates the need to tend to our personal relationships. They need to be cultivated, watered, and fertilized. If these necessities are ignored, they will wither and die.

No matter how important our professional work is, our spouses and children still need us. They need our attention, our appreciation, our praise, our concern, and our respect. They need to know we care about their lives just as we need to know they care about ours. Political life does not entitle anyone to one-way relationships. We cannot put our private lives on auto pilot.

Several years ago I was asked to be the keynote speaker at a dinner. I was to address the topic of protecting our private relationships while living within the Washington culture. Two hundred and fifty people were coming to this event. The numbers were small, but the group was comprised of generals, admirals, senators, congress persons, and some senior presidential appointees. So, when I awoke that morning, my mind was focused on what I would say. I was at home, but I had already checked out.

At 7:30 A.M., my five-year-old daughter awoke. She was wired, too. She knew it was a very special and big day. The night before, while I was counseling, she and her mother had gone out and purchased a new bike. When she awoke that morning she had only one agenda: to ride her new bike. It was important for her that I immediately come out that morning and look at it. She needed me to give her the spotlight. She needed me to get into her world and be excited with her. To her having a new bike is far more important and much more exciting than talking to a roomful of adults. So there we stood in the garage, looking, laughing, and talking about the most grand thing in her simple life, a new bike.

We need to remember that the things that occur in the lives of our spouses and children are just as important to them as the events in our lives are to us. If your daughter tries out for high school cheerleading or soccer and does not make the team, the disappointment and pain she feels will seem just as significant and intense to her as not being re-elected to Congress would feel to you.

If you have a son who just made varsity football or tennis, he is just as excited as you would be to receive a key committee assignment. We need to care enough to see the events of their lives *from their perspectives*. This only happens if you intentionally choose to focus your attention on your spouse and children.

When you give others the spotlight, you forget about yourself. This brief recess from the stress and priorities of your world, brings an unexpected refreshment and joy. Everyone wins. My kids are still at the age where they want to "do something" with me when I arrive home. Many days I feel so exhausted that playing is the last thing I want to do. But when I do my kids are satisfied, I am refreshed, and home feels like a great place to be after a tiring day. Pretty nice dividends.

I'm not saying these kinds of choices are easy. I know how difficult it is to balance our private and public lives—especially for members. And when I see members make a tough call, I take note. That's why I'll remember Steve for a long time.

Steve had been invited to the White House to attend a dinner with the president. But as the day arrived, Steve began to reflect on his life. He thought about his priorities, his recent schedule, the pace of his life, and his family. It struck him that lately he had not spent any significant time with his children. So, he did something that is almost unheard of in this town. He called the White House and asked them to inform the president that he would not be coming for dinner that evening . . . he needed to go home and spend time with his family. Then he called his wife and told her his decision.

He finished his day on the Hill and went home. When he got home he changed clothes and spent the evening talking and playing with his children. He never told them what he had canceled at the White House. His wife, however, had told the children about their father's decision to come home just to be with his family.

Finally, with bedtime approaching, one of his daughters could stand it no more. She went to her father and asked, "Dad, did you really give up having dinner with the president of the United States so that you could come home and have dinner with us?" The father looked at his daughter and simply replied, "That's right, Mary."

Let me ask you something. How do you think his children felt when they went to bed that night? They felt loved. They felt secure. They felt safe. They knew they were a significant priority in their parents' world. Something tells me that when they turned out the lights that evening, they all had a good night's sleep.

Think about It

The following questions are for your personal reflection. You may reflect on them alone or discuss them with your spouse, children, or a group of your peers.

1. How accustomed am I to being in the spotlight?

2. Do I know how to get out of the spotlight and give it away?

3. When was the last time I genuinely gave the spotlight to my spouse without hurrying to get it back? To my children? (Think about them one at a time by name, not as a group.)

4. How important has being in the spotlight become to me?

5. Can I still be content going to places if I am not given the spotlight?

6. Do I find that I get restless, bored, or withdrawn at an event if too much time elapses without me being at the center of attention?

CHAPTER 2

GET INTO THE
MUD PUDDLE

"Eyes that look are common. Eyes that see are rare."

—Anonymous

The next time you are at a political gathering, watch the eyes of the people with whom you are speaking. Few people will fix their gaze on you and hold it. Most, while trying to appear attentive, are keeping their eyes on what's happening in the rest of the room. While you speak they are trying to recall the name of the person coming their way, noticing who else is in the room, and listening in on other conversations.

If you want to be courageous, notice what *you* do with your eyes as you speak to people. What are you thinking about when someone else is speaking to you?

Members are masters at appearing interested and attentive, when in fact their minds and interests are miles away. And no wonder! All day long they have to listen to people drone on and on. It would take all my energy just to stay awake.

One Senate member told me how difficult it is to listen to others when he is campaigning. He described the struggle this way: "I show up at every event twenty minutes late and leave an hour early. Then I do the same thing at another event. While I am at the reception I am trying to make sure I meet the ten key people there whom I'm supposed to know, remember, and greet. Meanwhile I am trying to act unhurried and interested in everyone with whom I speak. Even when I want to listen carefully, it is not really possible."

Another member acknowledged the need to "keep moving" when meeting with people during a campaign. He mentioned that many members' conversational repertoire revolves around three questions: "What is your name? Where are you from? What do you do?" When at a reception many members ask a person those three questions, and then move on to the next person and ask the same questions. This continues until they've "worked the room."

I often kid members I know that being in Congress is perfect preparation for a career as a toll booth operator. Toll collectors only have time to say, "Hi. How are you? Good to see you. Have a nice day." After that they move on to the next individual, just like members at a reception. A steady diet of this would diminish anyone's ability to listen effectively.

Listening is far more rigorous than many people realize. It takes enormous mental energy to listen genuinely. When we listen well, we suspend our agendas and consciously focus on another person. Rather than think about what we are going to say next, we concentrate on the essence of what the other person is saying. No small feat, this is a wonderful skill and art to master. It results in people feeling understood, connected, close, and bonded.

Have you ever been with someone who is truly a skilled listener? Their eyes are so focused on you that you feel as though you are being x-rayed. You have no doubt that they are straining "to see" what you are saying. They are trying to catch the meaning of your words so that they have a sense of what you are saying, thinking, and feeling. No wonder someone has said, "A good listener is a silent flatterer." They flatter you with the respect shown via listening.

Bill Moyers is a superb interviewer in part because he is such an extraordinary listener. Watch one of his interviews sometime and study him rather than listen to the subject matter. Notice his eye contact, facial expressions, head posture, and movement. Everything about him communicates a genuine respect for the interviewee. His nonverbals suggest, "Go ahead, take your time, keep speaking. I am still interested, still earnestly listening, and still attempting to understand you fully." It is no mystery why his interviews are so revealing and contain such depth. People feel safe with him. They drop their guard and he is able to get into their world and understand it from their vantage point. Bill Moyers knows how to get into the mud puddle.

Let me explain this word picture.

Life has a way of knocking us down periodically. It is like running full speed in a football game and being "clotheslined" by a middle linebacker that we never saw coming at us. We may be too dazed to know what leveled us, but when our head clears, we find ourselves sitting on our rear-ends.

This is what I call getting knocked into the mud puddle of life. Lots of things can knock us into the mud puddle: reversals in health, relationships, finances, or careers are just a few of them. During difficult times people hunger for someone to get into the mud puddle with them. They need to be assured that someone else understands and cares about what they are experiencing.

Easier Said Than Done

This sounds deceptively simple. It is far more difficult than many people realize. Some believe they are very skilled at getting into another's mud puddle when, in fact, they have not even come close. This was true for me. For years I unknowingly did the wrong thing every time my wife Linda was knocked into the mud puddle of life. I thought I was helping her . . . I meant well. But despite my sincerity, what I did never worked.

My normal pattern would go like this. Something would happen to my wife which would "clothesline" her and throw her into the mud puddle. That evening she would want to tell me about it. All she wanted was for me to listen and understand what she felt. However, I never figured out that she usually did not need—and was not asking—me to do anything else. But that was too obvious and too easy. So, I tried to give her advice. I told her what she should do to get out of her predicament and how she could avoid the problem in the future.

When Linda tells me about something important to her, I classify it in one of three ways: as a problem, a question, or as if something is broken. My response is tailored to what I think I heard.

If I Think I Heard:	*I Respond With:*
1. A Problem ——————————>	*A Solution*
2. A Question ——————————>	*An Answer*
3. Something Is Broken ————>	*How to Fix It*

At times Linda relates something and it sounds to me like she is telling me about a problem. Now if my wife has a problem, I instinctively want to give her a solution. In fact, I give her my best solution. That just makes sense to me. If anyone comes to me with a problem, I assume they must want and need a solution.

I never helped Linda when I did this. Despite the wisdom and usefulness of my "solution," it was not what she needed or wanted. *She was not looking for a solution. She was looking for understanding.*

Other times Linda appears to be asking me a question. For example, when Linda is feeling stress about taking on too many projects, she asks, "Why did I say I would do this?" Grammatically, that is a question. Naturally, I want to answer her question. And once again I will give her my *best* answer. The trouble is she really doesn't want an answer. When I give her one, I miss the mark. She will not feel understood by me or connected with me.

The third way I misinterpret Linda's intent is when I think she is telling me about something that is "broken" in her life. I think she wants something fixed. When my wife feels discomfort, I want to help her. So guess what I do? Like the Shell Answer Man, I tell her how to fix that which is broken. I give her advice.

But it isn't helpful because it isn't what she needs.

After repeating this pattern countless times in my early

marriage, I began to realize something: I was missing the essence of what my wife was saying, wanting, and needing. (Talk about a quick study!)

One day, in a moment of emerging insight, I said to Linda, "Let me get this straight. When life knocks you into the mud puddle you may tell me your problem, but you do not want me to give you a solution at that time. Is that right?" With a look of surprise she responded, "That's right."

Sensing I was on a roll, I continued, "And when you are distressed about something you may seem as if you are asking me a question. You may even put it in the form of a question. But you really don't want me to give you an answer to your question. Is that right?" Now she looked at me with disbelief; as if I were beginning to awaken out of a long-term coma. Then she replied, "That's right."

I continued, "And when I think that you are telling me that something is broken, you actually don't want me to tell you how to fix it. Is that right?" By this time she had all the excitement that Ann Sullivan experienced at the water pump when she finally got through to Helen Keller. "That's right. You finally have it! I do not need or want your advice on how to get out of the mud puddle. Rather, I want you to just stop, sit down, and get into the mud puddle with me. And if you will do that it will become the solution and fix what is broken."

I sat back with the satisfaction of someone who had just solved a mystery or broken a secret code. I had discovered a large piece of the puzzle that could help Linda—and others—feel listened to and understood.

When life knocked Linda into the mud puddle, she did not want me to be a consultant. She did not want my wisdom at that moment. She did not want my advice. She simply wanted me to take the time to focus my attention on her and get into her world. She wanted me to *sit down in the mud puddle with her*. That was it. She needed me to listen to her so effectively that I would have a sense of what life looked and felt like to her at that moment. That day I saw how far I was from really helping my wife feel understood.

A Little Child Shall Lead Them

Since more men than women have a problem with this, I'm going to specifically address husbands here. Take the figure of speech I have been using and think about it literally. If you are a married man, think about your wife and your usual response or behavior when she is in the mud puddle. Picture her *literally* sitting in a mud puddle. As she shares her needs or struggles, what do you do?

Most men stand about thirty feet away from their mate while she is in the mud puddle. They carefully avoid going too near it. From this safe distance the husband shouts out his suggestions to his wife. The proposals he presents depend upon her concerns. Most men will do what I did: tell her how to fix what is broken, give her answers to her questions, or provide solutions to her problems. He doesn't go near the mud puddle. He is still safe, removed, and distant. He never has to get himself dirty.

On our best days, some of us men actually get up and walk toward the mud puddle (figuratively speaking). We move to the edge of it but carefully avoid getting into it. Then, in a moment of what we think is enormous compassion, we lean over, extend our hand to our wife, and try to pull her out of it without our ever stepping into it. We mean well. Our motives our good. Our methodology isn't. It doesn't work.

When I told a group of congressmen about this word picture, a member reminded me of the wonderful capacity young children have to do this. Children are astute and careful observers of their parents' lives. At times they can be refreshingly full of compassion and understanding.

The member went on to tell us about a memorable moment in his life. A seasoned veteran, he had lost his first race for Congress. He ran again and fully expected to win. The election came and he experienced what so many members dread: defeat. He was shocked.

Discouraged and depressed, all he could do for a few days was sit around the house in a daze. His young daughter, with her security blanket trailing along behind her, came out to talk and play with her dad while he was sitting on the couch. She wanted him to color with her, but got no response. He was oblivious to her.

Finally without saying a word, she sat down next to him and gently picked up his right arm and tucked her treasured security blanket under it. She put his arm back down, patted it lightly, and softly walked away. She was gone before her dad became aware of what she had done.

What had this little girl done? What did she say so beautifully through her actions? In her own precious and innocent way she was saying, "Dad, I'll get into the mud puddle with you. I don't know how to help, Dad. I am too young to understand what is happening. But I want you to know that your pain matters to me. I want you to know that I love you and care about you."

That's exactly what you and I need to do for our spouse and children. We need to slow down, get out of the spotlight, and get into their mud puddles. As our children grow older, we need to schedule time to ask them questions. Not questions that may make them feel spied upon and therefore defensive, but questions that show genuine interest in their lives, experiences, and well-being. When our children return from some event or experience (and it does not matter if they are five or thirty-five years old) they need us to ask, sincerely, "What was it like?"

When asked at the right time and in the right way, this question can have a surprisingly powerful effect. Verbally and nonverbally, you are telling your child, "I love you. I care about what you are doing. I give you my permission to paint your world for me. Take your time and paint it so well that I can see it, hear it, and feel it with you. I will do my best to feel as though I was with you in the experience that you describe. I want to share your successes and struggles, your victories and defeats."

What Do I Do Once I'm in the Mud Puddle?

Many people are motivated to get into someone else's mud puddle, but they don't always know what to do once they're there. They don't know what to listen for.

Let me suggest two questions to ponder when listening to your spouse or children:

1. What emotion is being shared?

2. On a scale of one to ten, how intense is this emotion?

These questions will help you focus on the essence of the

other person's experiences. They will help you identify the exact emotion being felt and how deeply it is felt. When you listen to them this way, your family will feel understood and not alone. They will intuitively sense that you have locked on to their broadcasting frequency. Their communication is being picked up by the one person they most want to tune in: their mate or their parent.

Making Focused Listening Manageable

People experience a wide range of emotions, but most can be grouped into one of six categories. (I do not mean to minimize the power of other emotions such as frustration, guilt, etc.) The six emotions to listen for are:

tenderness	fear
happiness	anger
excitement	sadness

Once we have identified the category of emotion, we can focus on the intensity of the emotion. When these two things are done, we are able to comprehend more fully the world of our spouse and children.

When you are listening, don't hesitate to ask questions. In order to zero in on someone's exact experience, you need the speaker's assistance. Questions bring the person's experience into focus. Good questions not only help us gain an accurate reading of someone's experience, they also help us avoid misreading the experience.

Don't Be Fooled!

It is particularly difficult to accurately read some men without asking questions about what they feel and how intensely they feel it. For numerous cultural and personal reasons, many men struggle with showing their emotions.

Imagine a member who has been waiting for a key committee assignment. He feels fairly confident about it. On the day of committee selection the votes are tallied and the assignments are made. He discovers he is not assigned to the committee he expected.

What do you think he is experiencing on the inside? At his gut level? If he is like many men the feelings he experiences on the inside may be vastly different from those he exhibits or expresses on the outside.

He's probably simultaneously experiencing three of the six emotions: fear, anger, and sadness. He's afraid because he wonders how this will play in his district. Will the media start to suggest that he is not a strong player on the Hill? Will his colleagues still have confidence in him? Are they beginning to write him off and not take him seriously? This fear (which stems from both vulnerability and insecurity) needs to be recognized by the member and anyone who really wants to get into his mud puddle.

He's also angry. Very angry. His anger may be at a friend who promised to back him but didn't. It may be at a colleague whom he believes stonewalled him in the vote. Or, it may be at himself. Additionally, his anger may act as a cover to prevent him from experiencing more vulnerable emotions such as fear and sadness.

Lastly, he's experiencing sadness. He has a sense of loss. He may feel betrayed and rejected. Or his sadness may come from temporarily feeling like a zero. He may be in grief.

Remember, you cannot assume you know the emotion or the intensity of another person's emotions—especially a man's. For instance, this member may go home or call his wife and tell her what happened. He may give her the basic data. But he may do it in such a nonchalant manner that his tone suggests that he doesn't care. He may look, act, and sound like this is no big deal. Yet his internal world is vastly incongruous with his external behavior. What he is *experiencing* is very different from what he is *exhibiting*.

Let's assume someone picks up on his disappointment. But if, on a scale of one to ten, this member is sad at a level of eight while acting as if it is only a three, then the casual observer does not think his pain is very intense. Therefore the observer probably will not pay much attention to it. Despite identifying the right category of emotion, they have missed him by a mile!

In order to double check the intensity of an emotion, the listener might ask, "You seem to be disappointed or saddened by this. Is that right?" If the answer is yes, they can then ask, "On a scale of one to ten, how intense is it?" At this point the member has the chance to fine tune the level of his experience for the listener. The member could say, "Actually, my sense of sadness is an eight." That is a very different level of sadness from level three. It should signal the listener to pay attention. Note that if the question wasn't asked, the speaker would not have volunteered the information and could easily have fooled even those who care about him.

Anger Alert

Of all the emotions, anger is the one men are often most free to experience and express. Men feel that they can show anger and still keep their maleness intact. Their ego is not disrupted by it. Consequently, men use anger to display a wide range of other emotions. It is often their inelegant way of admitting they are hurt and that they want help or closeness with someone.

But anger doesn't draw people to us, it drives them away. Anger rarely solicits compassion. People are not eager to get into the angry person's mud puddle. They want to run from—not toward—the person. Anger makes people want to leave rather than love. Wise individuals learn to articulate their needs and emotions through more than the roar of anger.

Practice Makes Perfect

My wife and I have worked hard at trying to identify our own and each other's emotions and their intensity. In the early years of our marriage, I often misread her. Linda and I represent our inner worlds very differently. Linda was raised in a family in which people rarely raised their voices. They always gave the appearance of calmness and composure. Even when she didn't feel calm, Linda would give all the outward signs of feeling calm and composed.

It was only after I concentrated on understanding what she was feeling that I realized the huge gulf between her external behavior and her inner thoughts and emotions. On occasion she might appear irritated with something I said or did. I would pick up on her anger but wrongly conclude that it was only an intensity of two or three. I wouldn't take it very seriously. Only after asking her about specific emotions and their intensity did I really learn to be aware of and sensitive to her world.

* * *

In this chapter we've talked a lot about the skill of careful and caring listening. Like all skills it needs to be both comprehended and practiced. Cultivating this skill enormously enriches a relationship. But if we are going to do this we also need to slow down the pace of our lives. We need to remember that *all healthy relationships are a function of schedule and skill.* The fact that we have perfected a skill does not matter if we never have time to use it.

When you start to perfect your ability to really listen to your spouse and children, you will discover that it radically changes your thinking and listening patterns in committee meetings, with colleagues, and with constituents. It will transform all your relationships.

Think about It

The following questions are for your personal reflection. You may reflect on them alone or discuss them with your spouse, children, or a group of your peers.

1. Does the pace and speed of my life prevent me from looking at the life in the lane next to me?

2. How willing am I to make looking at the lives around me (i.e. my family) a priority?

3. How skilled am I at getting into my family's mud puddle?

4. Do I remember what six emotions I need to listen for?

5. Do I understand why I need to inquire about the *category* and the *intensity* of emotion someone is experiencing?

6. Do life skills like these make me uncomfortable?

CHAPTER 3

HOW LONG CAN YOU HOLD YOUR BREATH?

"Hope deferred makes the heart sick,
but desire fulfilled is a tree of life."
—Proverbs 13:12

To a seventh grade boy it was a big event. A competition in front of the entire school between the seventh grade and the eighth grade.

Every gym class held a contest to see who could hold his breath the longest under water. The winner of one class challenged the winner of another class until, finally, one swimmer had defeated all the other winners and the school champion was declared.

Winning, especially as a seventh grader, gave me status and notoriety which lasted for almost forty-eight hours. (Which is about the same life span they have in Washington!) Everyone crowded around me, wanting to know, "How long can you hold your breath? How long can you stay under water? How long can you wait before you come screaming to the surface gasping for air, in need of refreshment and rejuvenation?"

As of the writing of this book, breath-holding contests are still not recognized as an Olympic event. They are not even announced in the "Weekend" section of the *Washington Post*. It is difficult to find one that you can go to and watch. But they are held all the time in Washington. Many members try to see how long their families can hold their breath and go without oxygen in their relationships before being forced to surface for air.

A practiced ear will hear members asking his or her spouse questions such as these:

How long can I be away traveling before you reach a point of exhaustion or exasperation?

How many nights per week can I be gone before you can no longer tolerate it?

How long can you go without affection, affirmation, or praise?

How long can you go without our having any time to talk honestly, communicate, and connect with each other?

How long can you go without sexual intimacy? (Or, how long can you go with our having time for sexual intimacy but no time for relational intimacy?)

How long can you go with no help with the children?

How long can you endure when I am so preoccupied with my career that I have no time, interest, or energy left to focus on you or the children?

How long can you survive when I am so spent by the time I arrive home that I am either irritable or exhausted and will therefore be unavailable for the evening or weekend?

How long can you live as if you are a single parent because I cannot be counted on to partake in the decisions, plans, needs, or responsibilities of keeping a family intact and organized?

How long can you hang on when I am married to my career and only have time for a fling with you?

What I really want to know is: How long can you endure when I am driven to be in the spotlight and have no time or desire to get into your (or the children's) mud puddle?

This contest rarely begins with a direct question or overt challenge about how long individuals can hold their breath. The beginning is usually subtle and difficult to detect. That is what makes it so insidious. Often, people are unaware that they are starving their spouses or children in areas of critical need—and the spouses and children are often reluctant to acknowledge that they have very pressing, real, and legitimate needs. They naively believe that the individual's career or responsibilities are so important that their own needs are no longer legitimate and should not be mentioned.

Things Will Settle Down Soon

People play the game of "holding their breath" most intensely when they land new jobs in Washington. The desire to excel makes them so focused that they put their family on hold. Usually it is not intentional neglect or abandonment. It is simple preoccupation. Additionally, everyone involved assumes that "it will only be for a little while . . ."

Whether it is a position as an administrative assistant, a diplomat, a presidential appointee, or a member of Congress, the pattern is the same: becoming so preoccupied with a new job in Washington that personal relationships suffer. These individuals desire to achieve, excel, and make their mark. They don't want to miss their "shot in the big leagues." They want to make a name for themselves as real contenders, real players—but in doing so, they bet the farm.

At this point couples agree to what could be called "the unwritten contract." This mutual agreement is not written out and it may not have been discussed. But there is an assumption or implied consent that the entire family is "in this together." Everyone purports to support the new opportunity.

If the unwritten contract were in writing it might look like this:

The Unwritten Contract

We agree that I have to be very busy at my new job for a while.

We understand that I need to get off to a good start and make favorable impressions.

We agree that I need to learn my new responsibilities and that I will therefore bury myself in my work while I am on a learning curve.

We concur that this is the most important opportunity I have had and I cannot blow it.

We admit that our entire future may pivot on my performance.

We understand I have to give my all to this new endeavor.

We understand that I will be preoccupied for a while.

We understand that I need to hear your support, but not your struggles.

(At this point in the contract the print gets much smaller.)

We understand that I cannot be there for you.

We understand that you might starve for my attention, assistance, affection, and affirmation.

We understand that I cannot get into your mud puddles.

We understand that you are essentially on your own.

We understand that I need you to hold your breath for as long as you can . . . and maybe even longer.

Signatures   _____   _____

                  Husband   Wife

                  _____   _____

                  Child   Child

That is a blunt contract. It spells out the hardships our families are often asked to endure so that we can succeed. Many times there are hidden costs. Washington is crowded with people who are staggered by the price they paid to chase a career opportunity. Families can avoid sticker shock when they know in advance the actual price they might pay for obtaining a goal.

Just recently I received a phone call from a man I do not know. Someone advised him to call me for information about life in Washington. Guess what this man is doing? He is leaving his life and work in a large midwestern city to take a position at the Justice Department. He told me, "I will be arriving in Washington on September 16. But my family will not move out here until January. This will give me the opportunity to focus on my new job and work long hours."

Did you catch that? Do you see what is happening? He is asking his family to hold their breath for a mere four months. (Of course that is no problem for his wife and their two children. She can handle her work along with the feeding, clothing, cleaning, driving, disciplining, supervising, comforting, teaching, and loving of the children. Along with these things, throw in getting them adjusted to school and through Halloween, Thanksgiving, and Christmas on her own. And in her own time she can keep the house perfectly clean to help sell it.)

They have already signed the contract! They have no idea how much it may cost them. But why worry about cost . . . this is his chance at the big time.

"I've Decided to Run for Congress"

People running for a seat in Congress or those in tight re-election races often agree to the unwritten contract—and later come to regret it. To understand why, let's take a closer look at a family during the campaign season.

Let's imagine a husband who decides to run for Congress. The initial stages of a campaign can be enjoyable for all family members. In the beginning the race has cost them very little in their lives or relationships. In fact, it often bonds the couple closer together. They are both focused on the campaign. They are both in support of it. (If the wife is resistant, she has not yet verbalized her feelings.) Both are excited and invigorated by the challenge and the initial taste of notoriety. Both are in agreement about the goal. Consequently, they have a sense of teamwork, an *esprit de corp*. They feel like a solid, confident team. They sense the feeling that "we're in this together." They feel enthused, strong, and solid.

They come out of the chute with a strong sense of unity. The candidate assumes his family is behind him for the duration of the race—and they have every intention of doing this. But as the campaign continues, their stamina begins to falter. They need oxygen, but want to appear as if they are feeling fine.

To avoid discouraging the candidate, the family may not initially mention their private struggles. They have been caught off guard. They underestimated how difficult this endeavor would be on them. They had not anticipated dad being gone every day for so long. They had not realized he'd be available to everyone but them. They had not expected his frequent forgetfulness regarding a speaking engagement he had accepted or his claims that his campaign staff had overbooked him. They had no way of knowing how often he would receive a last minute invitation to speak somewhere and that he would accept because some key people were attending. They had not foreseen how lonely life would be without him, how much the kids would miss him, and how many important family events he would miss because something that was important to the election had come up.

A Change of Heart

As this pattern emerges, the family experiences a change of heart. Their focus, energy, and excitement for the race diminish significantly. They grow weary of listening to the candidate only talk about his race, speeches, schedule, strategy, and polls. The campaign that once bonded them closer together is now driving them apart. Once eager to listen to the candidate talk about the campaign, they now resent hearing about it every day.

This change about the campaign could be put on a continuum. Families move from being:

Eager to be involved in the campaign
   to being
Eager to hear of the campaign
   to being
Politely tolerant when hearing of the campaign
   to being
Bored with campaign news
   to being
Indifferent to campaign news
   to being
Resentful of campaign news
   to being
Intolerant of campaign news.

Families lose zeal for the campaign because of its massive intrusion into their family. They fear it will consume their lives the way it has the candidate's. The family senses that their needs and priorities are very different from the candidate's:

The candidate is afraid of losing the election. The family is afraid of losing the candidate.

The candidate fears rejection at the polls. The family feels rejected by the candidate.

The candidate feels his family is insensitive to the pressure and stress he is under. The family feels the candidate is insensitive to the pressure and stress they are under.

The candidate feels the family does not understand him. The family feels he does not understand them.

The candidate is feeling alone. The family is feeling alone and abandoned.

When these divergent interpretations develop, most families, instead of moving to mutual understanding about each person's feelings and needs, simply move to isolation. They begin to withdraw, settle into their own worlds, and carve out their own way of surviving and meeting their needs elsewhere.

If they stay on this course, companionship will be traded for co-existence. Life partners will become roommates. At best the relationship will move from dynamic and meaningful to dull and mediocre. At worst, it will atrophy and die.

To avoid this and recreate the sensation of harmony, the candidate may try to reason with his wife. He may refer to the unwritten contract at this time and say things like, "Didn't we agree on this together?" or, "I thought we were in this together . . . that is what you said." Or he may say, "I thought you were going to be in my corner. Instead you are only on my case, and I don't need that right now."

The family must grasp what is happening in these moments. The candidate is *not comprehending* the family's pain or needs. Rather than validating the feelings, he does something else. He asks them to *ignore* their need for oxygen by reminding them of their past agreement. He appeals to an unwritten agreement that is now held up like a binding legal contract.

But this doesn't resolve anything because it completely misses what the family wants the candidate to see and do. They want him to slow down. They want him to understand their present experiences. They want him to know what they are experiencing emotionally and physically. They want him to get into their mud puddle.

The family knows they said they would try to support him in his election efforts, but they wish he would see that they said that when they felt strong, rested, and refreshed. Now that they are physically or emotionally depleted, they are incapable of keeping their promise. His appealing will not give them energy to go on in a lifestyle that keeps asking them indefinitely to hold their breath.

Any Reprieve Is Momentary

If the candidate is articulate and persuasive, he may be able to momentarily manipulate the spouse and family into believing that they are wrong to be frustrated or fatigued. He may use guilt-inducing statements such as, "Don't you realize the difficulties of a campaign? Don't you know how many people I have telling me what to do, where I need to go, how I need to improve, and what I need to say and how to say it? Don't you know how pressured I feel with people I need to call, money I need to raise, and campaign problems I need to solve? Why do you have to come to me with this now? Why are you always like cold water on my dreams?" (Note that most of these statements may be legitimate or true—but they steal the spotlight and place it on the candidate's needs.)

Comments similar to these may shame the family into retreat. The wife may feel guilty for imposing on his world—after all, the candidate does have so much on his mind. She may begin to think erroneously that her needs are not legitimate. She may think or even say, "Excuse me for my self awareness; I will try to stuff my needs, ignore them. Maybe they will go away. I cannot expect you to be there for me. I need to be there for you. I'm sorry. I'll try to be stronger. I'll try not to be a drain on you. I don't want to rain on your parade."

Neither manipulation by the candidate nor denial by the family will resolve this situation. Legitimate needs have to be met in legitimate ways. Ignoring them does not work over extended periods of time. People cannot hold their breath indefinitely even if they want to do so.

If after reading this chapter, you realize that you and your family have been holding your breath and are deprived of oxygen, you need to ask for help. You need to get the attention of your mate. An initial dialogue with a mate that is unaware of your needs might go as follows:

"There is something that I want to discuss with you. I want to know if this is a good time to talk or if we should do it later. Either time is okay with me as long as we do it."

When they decide to talk, the spouse might continue:

"I want you to know that I really am committed to you and your work. I genuinely want you to win. I want you to do well. I know how much this means to you. I remember my past agreement and promise of my support and commitment. I meant those things that I said and agreed to when this campaign began. But I need to have you understand what I am experiencing right now. Today.

"If I keep ignoring these thoughts and needs, it will greatly affect my ability to rejoice in your work and my sensitivity to your needs. I want to be able to continue to do that. To do so, I need you to understand what it is like here for me, and for us, when you are gone all the time.

"I would like for you to give me the spotlight. I need you to listen carefully so that you can understand my world as if you were in it. I am not attacking you. I only want to be understood by you. The one thing I most desire for you to understand is . . ."

At this point focus on the specific desire, need, struggle, or emotion you want to communicate. For example, you may mention your exhaustion, need for relief, aloneness, concern for the children's well-being, or self esteem. Your objective is to ask your preoccupied spouse to slow down and focus on *your life* in order to sense what life has been like for you or the children.

* * *

It is so easy to inadvertently test our families. We often ask them to hold their breath for outrageous periods of time. Or we ask them to agree to the unwritten contract. If couples and families are to flourish in a campaign environment, they must have the time, skill, and will to get out of the spotlight, get into each others' mud puddles, and recognize their need for oxygen.

Think about It

The following questions are for your personal reflection. You may reflect on them alone or discuss them with your spouse, children, or a group of your peers.

1. Have I been challenging my family to see how long they can hold their breath?

2. Who in my family most needs oxygen rejuvenation? What part can I play in their refreshment? What do they need from me?

3. On pages 46 and 47 there is a list of the various ways people play the game, "How Long Can You Hold Your Breath?" What are the two or three ways I am most likely to play this game?

4. Does this concept of the unwritten contract make sense? Have I asked anyone to sign it?

5. Has my family paid a price for me to be in a campaign?

6. Am I under such pressure that I react (rather than listen and respond) when my family tries to tell me about their lives and needs?

7. Are my family and I willing or able to keep living like this?

CHAPTER 4

THE HIDDEN MARATHON

"I've learned to look at people and say to myself,
'Nobody knows what they've been through.' "
—M. Scott Peck

January of every even-numbered year. For members of Congress it is more than the start of a new year. It dawns quietly, but you can sense it in the atmosphere. It is unmistakable, almost palpable. When it emerges fully it will dominate the life of each member while shaping the agenda and motivations of the full Congress.

It's called the campaign season.

The election races have no formal beginning, but every member hears the starting gun about this time. Re-election is underway. With it will come a distinct change in each member's life. His focus is different.

Even his conversations change: "What kind of race are you looking at? Do you have an opponent? Is he a serious challenge?

Can this opponent do any damage? Has he been able to raise any money? What kind of name I.D. does he have? Is he getting any press? How much will you need to raise for your race? What kind of campaign fund do you already have? What were your numbers in the last race? By what percentage did you win? Are you going to do a poll? How much will it cost?"

As the campaign season unfolds these questions will become more frequent and more intense. Members with tight races must pay attention to these issues and many more like them. For them, January is a wake-up call. Like a professional athlete whose off season is ending, January is the start of spring training. It is time to get in shape for the competition. A marathon has begun and it will not end until the first Tuesday in November. (For members with safe seats or no opponents, this season is a completely different experience.)

It is difficult for people who are not close to the political process to imagine what it is like to be a member of Congress in the midst of a difficult campaign. Everywhere they go, they are expected to entertain and enthrall. Their comments are revealing:

"I get so tired of hearing my own voice."

"I weary of saying the same thing over and over again."

"I hate asking people for money and then having to come back and ask them for more money."

"I am exhausted but I have to keep going. I cannot stop."

"Most people are very nice, but I cannot believe how rude or disrespectful some people can be."

"I enjoy people, but I'm sick of shaking hands, making small talk, telling the same jokes, and answering the same questions."

"Do you have any new jokes I can use?"

They may mention the unpleasantness of entering a smoke-filled hall where people have been drinking long before the member arrives. Or they may mention how difficult it is, at the end of a long day, to endure waiting their turn to speak at an event that is already one hour behind schedule.

Even more difficult is the struggle to accommodate three diverse groups: the Washington staff, the campaign staff, and their family. Each group wants the member to do something different. The Washington staff wants the member to pay attention to current political issues, upcoming votes, committee meetings, visiting constituents, and keeping the Hill staff focused. The campaign staff wants him to spend more time out in the district, be more visible, and to do more campaigning, speaking, and fund raising. His family insists he spend some uninterrupted time with them. As the race progresses, many members put their personal lives on hold. They no longer feel in charge of their own schedules or lives.

This can be madness. Election races can be grueling marathons. I have considerable respect and sympathy for all members that endure them.

The Loneliness of the Long Distance Runner

Recently I had lunch with Larry, a member involved in a difficult campaign. I was reminded of how easy it is for members to forget what their campaign lifestyle does to a spouse and family. Larry talked about how difficult it is for him to hustle several days a week in Washington. He squeezes all the usual things into his schedule: meetings with his staff and constituents, attendance at his full and subcommittee meetings, running over for votes, doing the necessary receptions and interviews, making phone calls, checking correspondence, preparing speeches, and the things that pop up unexpectedly each week. Then, immediately after the last vote on Thursday or Friday he has to jump on a plane and travel cross-country to his district. He is out on the stump the entire weekend and then returns by a red-eye flight to D.C. to be present for the first vote of the new week. Then he starts the cycle all over again.

While commiserating with Larry about the difficulty of this lifestyle, I asked him how his wife was doing in her race. He had no idea what I meant. He looked inquisitively at me to see if I was joking. When he realized I wasn't, he asked me what I meant. I mentioned that his wife was running a marathon, too, and that hers may be more difficult than his.

Two Very Different Races

My comments caught him off guard and he asked me to explain what I meant. As we continued, I talked about the difference between the marathon run by a member and the one run by the spouse.

Running the marathon for public office is hardly a solo event. It is well publicized, organized, and observable. The runner is surrounded by professional coaches, trainers, friends, acquaintances, fans, volunteers, public relations experts, media people, and countless support personnel who are there to make his run more enjoyable and successful.

As he runs his 26.2 miles he is never alone. At the starting line he is surrounded by family, friends, staff, well-wishers, and media. His send off makes him feel strong, supported, and confident. He starts out with high spirits and a good stride.

He has mile markers along the way and people to care for his needs. As he runs, people on the sidelines cheer him toward the finish. They urge him on and tell him to finish the race because his victory is so needed. Like adrenaline to his system, their words of affirmation drive him, giving him energy. They numb any discomfort he feels and give him the ego strength to continue.

When weariness or heat exhaustion set in, people hand him cups of cold water or towels as he runs by them. He never has to face his pain alone. Between his staff and supporters, someone is always there for him. They care for him, encourage him, exhort him, and do whatever else is necessary to keep him running effectively.

As the race nears the finish line, the member is surrounded by more and more people. (Especially if it appears his victory is certain.) He draws strength and resolve from these people. Their approval, praise, and applause sustain him. Like Jimmy Connors at the 1991 U.S. Open, the member is invigorated by the reaction of the crowd.

As the member approaches the finish line, the streets are lined with thousands of cheering people that are pulling for him. Like a Masters champion walking up to the eighteenth green at Augusta, he senses he is the man of the moment. All eyes are on him and he wants to finish with style. He forgets his fatigue in the joy of the moment. When he breaks through the tape as the winner, the crowd explodes with applause in unison.

As he heads to the winner's circle the applause continues. People near him shout "at-a-boy" and "way to go" and those closest to him give him hugs, handshakes, and high-fives as he works his way through the crowd. The exhilaration of winning makes all his effort and exhaustion worthwhile. It's moments like these that keep him signed up for a new marathon every other year or every six years. He knows that moments like this are not found in the corporate world.

Meanwhile, back at the proverbial ranch and unknown to the member, his wife runs her marathon. Hers was just as long as his and just as difficult—but hers was run in private. It was run in back alleys. No crowds launched her at the start of the race. There was no one to fire her up and motivate her to hit a good stride. It was simply time to begin, so she left the starting block.

When fatigue or exhaustion began to affect her, no one was there to assist, encourage, or exhort her. No one was at the mile markers to shout words of comfort. No one let her know they cared about her. No one said they know how tough it is to run a marathon. No one gave her advice or assistance. No one offered her cold water, towels, or Gatorade. No medics stood nearby in case she experienced heat exhaustion or cramps.

At the twenty-mile marker she hit the wall. Her body screamed for rest and refreshment. Her mind taunted her to quit and find relief. She struggled on, alone . . . still running a marathon that was hidden from public view.

The privacy of her race became poignantly clear at the finish line. When she crossed the 26.2-mile marker nobody cheered. Nobody noticed. Nobody cared. There was no encouragement. There was no help. There was no winner's circle, no awards, no applause, no hugs or high-fives. She finished . . . exhausted, alone, and unrecognized.

All along what had secretly sustained this runner was the hope that her husband would notice her sacrifice. She had hoped he would be aware of the loneliness and difficulty of her back-alley marathon. She had hoped he would acknowledge the necessity and importance of her race to him and their family. She had hoped he would pour honor and recognition upon her as a winner. She had hoped he would love her and thank her for her efforts.

But he didn't.

He was too excited about being in the winner's circle.

No Cakewalk for a Spouse

When I finished my explanation, Larry just looked at me. Silently. We both knew that if he spoke up he would break down. (Humanity of that depth is not displayed in the middle of the member's dining room.)

Larry recognized that his wife's race was every bit as tough as his. For the first time he realized that she was a pretty extraordinary athlete to keep pace with his life and work. The campaign season is no cakewalk for the spouse.

After a few moments he thanked me for helping him slow down and look at the runner in the lane next to him. He realized that he loved and admired who and what he saw there.

* * *

I can't close this chapter without acknowledging that members who have run in difficult races might claim that I have painted a picture that is inaccurate. I would agree that in some cases the race is very difficult, an uphill battle with hostility and criticism. And the victory is not always as grand as I made it appear.

However I wanted to shake members into realizing how difficult political life can be on their spouses. Men in general—and members in particular—are eager for someone to talk to them straight up. For many years I have watched as staffs, friends, and families of members do back flips to avoid upsetting the members. Their goal is to keep the members calm or happy rather than helping them grow and mature as human beings. They enable the members to live with their blind spots and weaknesses.

I'm not interested in being an enabler. I want to help members win in their private lives while serving in public office.

Members don't need another yes man, they need a friend who cares enough to be honest with them. As a politician, King Solomon knew what he was talking about when he wrote, "Faithful are the wounds of a friend. Profuse are the kisses of an enemy."

Think about It

The following questions are for your personal reflection. You may reflect on them alone or discuss them with your spouse, children, or a group of your peers.

1. Do you agree with the word picture that some election races are like running a marathon?

2. Do you agree that the spouse and family of a member also run a marathon?

3. Do you agree that the spouse runs a private marathon in the "back alleys"?

4. What do you think are the most difficult aspects of a member's race? What are the most enjoyable aspects?

5. What are the most difficult aspects of the spouse's race? The most enjoyable?

6. What does my spouse most need me to understand?

7. How can I make his or her marathon more bearable?

CHAPTER 5

PROFESSIONALLY FRIENDLY, PERSONALLY FRIENDLESS

"If you want a friend in Washington buy a dog."
—President Harry S. Truman

Truman's sardonic quip carries much truth. Friendship is a lost art for many in the political world or the Washington community. Experts at making a good first impression, people on Capitol Hill can dazzle a crowd. When you meet these people at some event, you feel you have known them for years. They seem so relaxed, friendly, and fun.

But after being with these same people year after year you discover that you really don't know them any better than you did after your first few visits with them. Careful not to let others into their lives or to let information about themselves out, they keep their guard up and play their cards close. They are delightful to be with but difficult to get to know.

Friendships within Washington's political community are not easily developed or sustained. Existing friendships are often neglected because people are too busy. Potential new relationships are not pursued because of lack of time and also lack of trust. Consequently, Washington is full of people who are professionally friendly and personally friendless. Some have theorized that the longer people stay involved in political life, the more their capacity for genuine relationships diminishes.

Note the struggle and honesty of the following comments:

"I do not have a single friend in Congress." (From a member with eight years of experience.)

"I have been in Congress for over ten years. After all these years, I don't believe there are six people who would care if I left Washington and never returned."

"The Senate is the most unfriendly place I have ever been. There is no such thing as the Senate Club. Senators are some of the loneliest people I have ever known." (Reflections from a U.S. Senator.)

"One thing I have learned is that there are no small enemies in Washington." (From a former member who retired after untruths spread about his life could not be stopped.)

"When senators get together, they all try to see who can be the most senatorial rather than just be themselves." (From a senior senator.)

A Recipe for Friendship

Several of the principal ingredients of friendship are portrayed in the film, *Driving Miss Daisy.* This movie depicts two unlikely candidates for friendship who unexpectedly are thrust together as a chauffeur and an aging widow. The story unfolds with the years and decades passing by as the two characters remain together as employer and employee. Something exceptional begins to emerge as these two people end up spending years of their lives together.

Miss Daisy is an old, frail woman. In one of the most poignant moments in the film, she is talking once again with her driver. Miss Daisy turns to him and spontaneously declares with surprise and gratitude, "Hoke, you're my best friend."

What happened in their relationship to result in her declaration? How did they become best friends? They spent sizable chunks of *time* together. They learned to *trust* each other. And they learned to *take the initiative in meaningful disclosure* with the other.

Any genuine and deep relationship must have these three ingredients. Without these the relationship lacks substance. It may be pleasant. It may be fun and enjoyable. It may appear natural and easy. But it will not be vital, dynamic, and healthy.

Time Is of the Essence

Some of the most enjoyable friends my wife and I have are members of Congress. But to keep our friendships alive—and to keep our own marriage alive—Linda and I are always fighting a shortage of this magical and elusive thing called time. We never have enough time—let alone extra time. Consequently, we regularly have to make decisions about parceling out the limited time we do have. It is not an easy call.

People in politics spend the majority of their time doing things that are obligatory or so special that they should not be missed. Any remaining discretionary time has many demands upon it—and the rest is consumed by the tasks of daily life.

People tell me that they want time for their friends and friendships, but when the weekend arrives, they are too physically and mentally fatigued. All they want to do is recover from the week that just ended and regroup for the upcoming week. Their tiredness and stress cause them to seek rest rather than relationships. It leads to isolation. (Some members spend their weekends working. They are so busy with political events in their district or state that they make little time to be with their family and friends.)

Interruptions . . . or Refreshment?

The speed and pressure of professional and political life can twist our sense of what is important. It is easy to become so preoccupied with our work that we become oblivious to those around us. And, if a friend should stop by or phone us, we view them as an interruption rather than a brief recess and source of refreshment from our work.

I saw my own failure in this area recently. A friend, who happens to be a member, called me in the middle of my work day. He caught me at a moment when I was engrossed in some research. Mentally I was miles away. Making time for a friend or small talk was the last thing on my mind. So after picking up the phone and talking for about forty-five seconds, I asked point blank: "What did you call me for, Scott? What do you need?"

He simply stated, "I didn't call you for anything special, Tom. I just called to see how you are doing. You have been on my mind." As we continued our conversation I held the phone with one hand and kept trying to wipe the egg off my face with the other. I had forgotten one of the most special aspects of friendship: Friends can call each other just because they care. They do not need a reason or an appointment.

Life in Washington makes many of us forget this simple truth. We lose sight of the value and joy of having—and being—a friend. We are so busy tackling what's urgent, we neglect what's important in life. We forget that "the most important things in life are not things."

Many busy or driven people could benefit from the sagacity of a member who stated, "I never met a businessperson who said on their death bed, 'I wish I had spent more time with my business.' " None of us will say that either. The trick is to remember this principle while there is still time to apply it.

Skittish and Gun-Shy

Trust, the second ingredient of healthy relationships, is often in short supply in Washington. Political survival often hinges on trading the capacity to trust others for the ability to be cautious and calculating. After learning the hard way that "there are no small enemies in Washington," members learn to play it safe. They learn to dialogue without disclosure. They learn to converse with others while not connecting with them. They learn to be polite while not being personal. They allow others to see their image without ever letting them into their inner world. They present their persona . . . but they will rarely let anyone meet their person.

This guardedness would be clinically notable in the normal population, but it is a necessary survival skill for politicians. Members quickly learn one of the axioms of political life: "Never say anything to anyone that you are not willing to have printed on the front page of the *Washington Post* the next day." This rule of thumb may be good for political survival, but it's expensive in personal relationships. It means that you cannot be yourself. You are not free to talk casually or spontaneously. Every word must be carefully weighed because it might be misconstrued or used against you.

The impact of living in a chronic state of guardedness is significant. Some people live with their guard up for so long that they lose the ability to take it down. Politicians are like police officers exposed to situations that are so extremely dangerous that they need to wear bulletproof vests for self-protection. Over time these officers may go home to an environment that is genuinely safe, loving, and nurturing. But they don't trust it. They are so acclimated to a state of "alert" that it becomes difficult to simply rest, trust, and unwind. Their sense of a safe place is lost and they are irritable, anxious, or withdrawn even when at home. They don't know how to take off the bulletproof vest even when it is no longer necessary.

Many members wish they could wear a bulletproof vest—especially of late. They are often shot at or attacked with a fierceness that is inappropriate and abusive. When elected, members are given a lapel pin that indicates they are a member of Congress. Many joke that their lapel pin must "look like a target or a bullseye to be shot at" because as members of Congress they are viewed as fair game for anyone who wants to take a shot at them.

Currently there is an open season on members, and they are considered the ultimate big game trophy by many hunters. There are no rules or guidelines to this hunt and no license is required. They may be hunted by any method, at any time, and in any place. In the end it does not matter if the member is killed, wounded, or maimed. Nor does it matter what happens to the member's family. All that matters is that they are struck down. Since politicians are viewed as big game, they are also considered fair game.

The hunters who are most feared are those in the media. Members have learned that "when reporters smell blood," they will not let go. Many journalists pursue their prey with relentless determination. If their quarry cannot be easily downed, they might go to great lengths to bait them and set traps that are unavoidable. Some of these hunters act as if bringing down a world-class trophy, such as a senator, would be a story they would relish for the remainder of their lives . . . even if the hunt had to be rigged a little to ensure its success.

I have seen numerous "trophies" politically killed or personally wounded by hunters using a gun called the media, shooting bullets called untruths. Like any animal that has been hunted too much, the species called "member of the United States Congress" has become wary. They are skittish and gun-shy. They have little means of protecting themselves against this potential predator should it decide to turn on them. As a result they become more guarded and less trusting. Eventually this lack of trust permeates their lives. (Where are the animal rights activists when you need them?)

Undoubtedly, the above analogy will provoke many legitimate thoughts and comments. Some members bring on their own demise. The media can play a proper and legitimate investigative role. Members and potential members shoot each other with more viciousness than the media use. But, as a counselor, I am more intrigued with the unconscious or underlying motives of the press (regardless of their legitimate sounding rationale) and with the resulting relational impact of these investigations on members, their families, and their friendships.

Washington's Game: Power or Proximity

Members can never be sure why someone wants to be their friend. They always wonder, "Do you like me as a person or because I am a political figure? Do you like me or do you just like to be seen with me? Will you still be as gracious and friendly to me when I am no longer in office, or does your interest expire with my term?"

Thousands of people in Washington play a game which revolves around two things that each player wants: power and proximity. Players either want to *be* the person in power or they want to be in *close proximity* to the person in power. People invest entire careers in obtaining one of these two options. A rather sad game when examined closely, it results in many people sacrificing valuable things for obtaining a goal that is, at best, temporary, elusive, full of illusion, and rarely satisfying.

While many members play this game, they have difficulty admitting to themselves that it is true. They want to believe that they are liked and well-received because of who they are as a person rather than because of their position. Yet, at a deeper level, they know that many people are feigning interest, warmth, and availability to them *only* because they are a member. When their last term ends, 98 percent of the people that are now so responsive to them will exit.

Sue told me she repeatedly reminds herself and her colleagues, "There is nothing more 'ex' than an ex member of Congress." She is acknowledging that this offer of friendship, praise, and respect from so many is available for a limited time only. It is generally not to be taken seriously or believed. She further muses, "Before I was a member of Congress, nobody cared about anything I had to say. Now that I am a member, people write down everything I say."

After playing this game every day, members become suspicious of those few who genuinely desire to be their friend. They become so accustomed to people wanting to be with them because of an agenda, something they need done, or an ulterior motive, that they stop looking for the offer of friendship with no strings attached. On those rare occasions when it does come along, they don't recognize it, or out of habit, they reject it. While staying alert to the occasional opportunity of a genuine friendship, members also need to go out of their way to maintain their old friendships. Let's explore why.

Taking the Initiative to Disclose

When members are elected to Congress, many of their genuine friends will suddenly make new assumptions about the relationship. They intuitively sense a major paradigm shift. They assume the rules of the relationship have changed. Often, they will look to the member for what the new rules are. They wonder if the new-found success will change the member and their right of friendship with them. They may think:

Now that you are in Congress you are much too busy to have time for us to get together for some relaxation and fun.

Now that you are in Congress you are too busy for me to call and "just shoot the breeze" with you. I now need a reason to speak with you. If my call isn't important, I should not interrupt you because you are busy handling national affairs.

Now that you are a member you have a new "status." You are in a different league than I. I'm not sure I feel as free to be your friend. Maybe you have outgrown me.

I don't think you have outgrown me. But I am waiting to see if you have the illusion of having outgrown your roots and friends. I will wait for you to make the first move. I want to know if going to Washington has gone to your head.

Members who don't anticipate their friends' reactions are often hurt when they stop calling or inviting them to places or events. The wise member understands that the old friends backed off because of uncertainty or insecurity—not because they no longer care about the member. Uncertainty has immobilized them.

Only the member can keep this perception from getting out of control. If they don't manage this well, they can end up even more friendless than is necessary. To their own peril, many members foster the illusion that they are indeed busy doing important and exciting things. At first this may pump up an insecure ego, but in the end it will leave the member with fewer calls and less time with those people who like him for who he really is.

Wise members go out of their way to assure their long-standing friends that they are still wanted, needed, and enjoyed as friends. Rather than wait for their friends to bring up the subject, the prudent member takes the initiative.

But over time members can become so accustomed to people doing things for them, arranging things for them, and accommodating them that they become takers and not givers. When members lose sight of the games played in Washington, they can begin to take seriously their treatment as royalty by staffers, lobbyists, and Capitol Hill workers. After awhile some members begin to act the way they are treated. They appear to think, "I am very near royalty and not far from deity." But they forget they are still profoundly human. They still need friends whom they can be with, laugh with, talk with, and confide in on a personal level.

Members would do well to remember that one of the laws of physics also applies to relationships: There is no such thing as perpetual motion. It does not exist in the natural world, and it does not exist in relationships. Relationships cannot sustain themselves. They can only be sustained by work and effort. When we stop taking the initiative in any relationship, the relationship will atrophy and then it will begin to die. Even people of prominence are subject to this phenomenon.

Political life does not exempt anyone from the most basic elements of friendship. They still require time, trust, and taking the initiative to disclose.

Think about It

The following questions are for your personal reflection. You may reflect on them alone or discuss them with your spouse, children, or a group of your peers.

1. Tom writes, "Washington is a city full of people who are professionally friendly and personally friendless." What do you think about this statement?

2. Have you found it easy to make friends (not friendly acquaintances) in Washington?

3. Time, trust, and taking the initiative to share, are listed as three important ingredients of friendship. Do you agree with this? What other factors do you believe are important?

4. Has political life affected your ability to manage friendships? How?

5. Has your capacity to trust others changed since entering political life?

6. Do you have friends that you trust enough to share with? Who are they? When was the last time you shared anything "risky" with them?

CHAPTER 6

PRAISE AND PEDESTALS, FANS OR FRIENDS

*"A friend is someone who doubles your
joy and divides your sorrow."*

He is one of my favorite people. He's exceptionally bright, highly verbal, and always straightforward. He called me from his district during an August recess just to hear how I had been doing. Then he asked me one of his typically pointed questions: "How many other members have called you during this recess?"

When I told him he retorted, "Tom, don't think that members are your friends. Most members don't know how to be a friend."

I didn't want to believe his comment, but he made me think.

Is this true? If so, why? Are there some hidden dynamics of political life that might be underlying causes for this situation?

Private Motivations in a Public World

All of us live with what one great leader called, "the malady of mixed motives." There are the ostensible reasons for doing things—and then there are the *real* reasons. Let's take a look at what motivates most members:

Overtly they are concerned about the welfare of the nation. Covertly they are concerned about their own well-being.

There is the purported noble and magnanimous commitment to the country. And there is the private management of a career.

There is the appearance of altruism. And there is private ambition.

There is the political rationale. And there is the private reasoning.

Most seasoned members will admit they have observed the power of private motivations in the political world. For example, they may have seen major pieces of legislation stopped or stalled because one member didn't like one of the key sponsors of the legislation. Naturally, members will cloak their motivation in legitimate-sounding rhetoric, but it is only a cover. As one member told me, "I have seen billion-dollar programs stopped because one member says of another member, 'I can't stand that S.O.B.' "

Jewish history contains a powerful illustration of private motivations cloaked in publicly acceptable arguments. The book of Esther tells the story. The scenario involves a king's highest and most trusted advisor named Haman. His modern equivalent would be the president's chief of staff.

Haman's career had been on a roll. He had power, prominence, and prestige. A personal friend of the king, Haman was clearly recognized as a big player in the political game. This guy had made it into the inner circle. The king had even ordered the palace servants to bow down to Haman when he rode by them.

There was just one thing that stuck in Haman's craw—an obscure servant who would not bow down to him when he rode by. Despite all his success, status, and power, his fragile ego could not handle a nobody who would not bow down to him. Haman was "filled with fury." His joy was stolen, his day was ruined, and his confidence rattled because of this guy who would not act impressed with him. (Haman is the classic example of what happens when an individual's career develops more than his character; when his political power is greater than his personal maturity. It's a dangerous combination.)

Upon further investigation Haman learns the guy's name is Mordecai and that he is a Jew. So Haman goes to the king with a plan to do this fellow in. While he is at it, he decides to wipe out all of the Jewish people. Notice Haman's explanation to the king about these people:

> Then Haman said to King Ahasuerus, "There is a certain people scattered abroad and dispersed among the peoples in all the provinces of your kingdom; their laws are different from those of every other people, and they do not keep the king's laws, so that it is not for the king's profit to tolerate them. If it please the king, let it be decreed that they be destroyed (Esther 3:8-9).

Haman sounds sincerely concerned about the king and the nation. His rationale seems so plausible. He claims that these people are everywhere (it is a national problem); they are different (and therefore dangerous); they do not keep the king's commands (they are insurrectionists); and they are not profitable (an economic liability). But, underneath all of this, is a man driven by a very private agenda. He is angry, insecure, and seeking vengeance on one individual. There is a vast disparity between his overt rationale and his covert motivations. Haman is an extreme example of a politician with hidden motives that drive him in his political life.

However, the power and prestige of Washington can—and does—seduce people into thinking they deserve to be on the pedestal. People in Congress are elevated, exalted, honored. They are viewed as larger than life and are granted a little more stature, a little more authority, a little more respect or credibility than is common.

Like Haman, many members find such automatic status difficult to resist. This can be a fatal mistake.

The Pedestal's Seductive Power

Let's look more closely at why people should be cautious of the praise and pedestals offered to them.

Some members become addicted to praise. Many members privately admit that being put on the pedestal or given the spotlight is the most gratifying part of their job. This is the payoff that makes all of their hard work worthwhile. The salary doesn't keep them in Congress, but the status and strokes do. They know that these will never be found in this measure anywhere else. So they stay in their jobs.

One member succinctly stated: "Status and affirmation are the drugs of choice for people in Congress." His point is that members, at a private level, are motivated, energized, and fueled by the approval and affirmation of others. This is what they live for; this is what keeps them going. Over time some become addicted to this praise given so freely and frequently.

Members who are hooked on the effects of praise will not do anything that will risk their seats in Congress. To do so would cut them off from the praise they can no longer live without. As one member mentioned, "This is why so many members who have been defeated try to run for Congress again. They miss the affirmation and praise of the crowds." They are attempting to return to their addiction.[1]

Some members resent the reality of home life after massive doses of praise and large amounts of time on a pedestal. Although members are given special treatment when out in public, it's a different story when they walk in the door at night. Those who can't make the transition from the unreal world of Capitol Hill to the real world of family relationships are in danger at this point. Instead of recognizing the unique treatment accorded them by their title, they resent being treated like everyone else when they arrive home. Some are indignant and incensed. They forget that the respect given to them on the Hill does not have to be won—it's protocol. At home it has to be earned.

This is an important truth for anyone who is praised and elevated in their professional world. We will explore it more fully in a later chapter.

Some members lose the ability to be real or genuine after accepting a place on the pedestal. Sometimes the pedestal makes people appear different than they actually are. These people pay an enormous price. Those who continue to play the role assigned to them eventually lose the freedom to be themselves. They lose the capacity to be authentically human. They discount that, like all of us, they need comfort, counsel, and companionship. They forget that, like all of us, they have hopes that are not realized, hurts that don't go away, and questions they would like to discuss.

Instead of finding themselves, they lose themselves.

At first prominence and prestige seem good. They are affirming and seem to strengthen the individual. They appear to build ego-strength and self-confidence. The person feels good about himself or herself because others seem to suggest that this is warranted. But when people are placed on a pedestal they do not anticipate one thing: the ladder to the pedestal is eventually removed—and there's no way down. Gone is the freedom to be a regular person, one of the crowd.

The pedestal, once so enticing and so eagerly climbed, begins to feel lonely, phony, and much less enjoyable. What started out as a position of honor has become a tiny prison of secret isolation. The pedestal keeps them quarantined. Genuine interaction with others is denied.

Wise is the member who accepts the honor, enjoys it, and wears it graciously, responsibly, . . . and casually. One day the pedestal will be handed to another. If you aren't addicted to it, the walk away will be easy. If you are addicted, the walk away will be filled with the pain of withdrawal.

Bump and Run Friends

Some who come to Washington find that the city suits them just fine. They like the frenetic, hectic lifestyle. They don't feel the culture prevents genuine relationships, they feel it *protects* them from having genuine relationships. These individuals do not want close or deep relationships. They have little idea what it is to have or be a friend.

The very thought of taking time to talk honestly with, or listen to, another individual is foreign to them. It seems unnecessary, unsafe, and unwise. They are undaunted by enormous responsibility, but deep within themselves they are terrified of real relationships. They are like the corporate sales woman who told me, "I like to stay in sales because I have to stay in contact with many people, but I don't have to connect with anyone. I never have to get close to people or let them get close to me."

I call this the bump and run strategy of life. Some members want to touch base and check in with people but they don't want tenderness or intimacy with them. As one senator mentioned: "Most members don't want personal relationships. They prefer superficial relationships. Members go to great lengths to hide any weaknesses. Congress offers you the perfect excuse of appearing compassionate in a generic sense while never making you get personally involved in real, tangible caring."

Sadly, some members confuse having fans with having friends. They assume a crowd is as good as a friend. All they want is for someone to listen approvingly to them or look admiringly at them. For them, recognition is more valuable than relationship. They desire fame more than friendship.

Capitol Hill is a safe haven for these people. It allows them the illusion of many friends, much stimulation, full schedules, important agendas, and vital meetings. It also protects them from facing their loneliness and fear of intimacy. They can tell themselves they are involved in relationships without ever troubling themselves with the risks and responsibilities inherent in any healthy relationship.

Those members with real political power (there are only a few of them) are most susceptible to this world of illusion. One member recognized that as a member of Congress you "automatically surround yourself with people who are paid to affirm you and your ideas." If some members knew what other members and staff actually think of them they would be devastated.

Think about it. I know a member who has exceptional support for his legislation and excellent attendance at his receptions by other members. Why is the attendance high? Because they view him as a friend? No. Some don't even like him personally or respect him. People go to his events and support his legislation because they do not want him to be angry with them. This member takes note of who attends his events and who does not, who is on time and who is late. One member who had the courage to stop playing games with this individual told me, "It is absolutely demeaning for members to show up at his events."

Few people challenge this person. His proposals cost the country hundreds of millions of dollars. But the other members will not risk having him use his power against them at a future date. So, his bills are supported, his illusions are sustained, and his colleagues are turned into frauds as they play the role of friend. And the country picks up the tab for this little charade called politicking.

Any intimacy and friendship this person has is an illusion. When his power is gone he will reel from the painful reality of how thoroughly disliked he was as a human being . . . as a person . . . as an individual.

The title of Mr. Chairman provides him with a bubble of protection. When the bubble bursts, the instant support for his ideas, the feigned admiration for his stories, the excessive laughter at his jokes, and the tolerance for his belligerence and immaturity will disintegrate. His position keeps reality at bay. It protects him from the uncomfortable intrusion of truth into his life . . . the truth about his person, his personality, his pathology.

No one wants to tell the emperor that he has no clothes. When the title of emperor is gone, so too will be the crowds, cronies, and the supposed fans and friends.

Down deep most members acknowledge that their position, not their person, gives them a place of notoriety. Those who are psychologically healthy are comfortable with this. But for others, knowing this truth makes them terrified of leaving their seats and keeps many here long after their usefulness is gone. They are afraid of the void which will follow once their title is taken away. Afraid, they stall as long as they can.

They become the "old-timers" who remain in Congress far too long. Congress no longer needs them. They need Congress.

No question about it, for those who want fame more than friends; respect more than relationship; power and influence more than personal relationships and intimacy, Washington offers them a unique opportunity. But in time the honest member recognizes that the praise gets old, the pedestal is lonely and uncomfortable, and the fans are friendly, but they are not friends.

Where do you see yourself in this chapter? What brought you to your job and why do you stay? How much do you need the praise? The pedestal? What price have you paid? Do you have fans or friends? Do you like what you see? Is this what you want?

Remember, it's never too late to change.

Note

1. A new political climate is developing. Many members are beginning to report that the moments of being on a pedestal and drinking in praise are being offset by the hostility and abuse they are receiving. More and more members are thinking and saying, "This job isn't worth it."

Think about It

The following questions are for your personal reflection. You may reflect on them alone or discuss them with your spouse, children, or a group of your peers.

1. Do I want fame more than I want friends?

2. Do I know what it is to have a friend? To be a friend?

3. Do people feel safe sharing their successes and struggles with me?

4. "A friend is someone who doubles your joy and divides your sorrow." Do I let anyone carry my struggles? Who do I share my struggles with?

5. When was the last time I genuinely dropped my guard with a friend and told him what I was thinking and experiencing?

6. What are the names of the three people whom I consider my closest friends? Have I ever thanked them for their friendship? Have I ever told them that I need and appreciate them?

7. Who do I want to call or write today to tell them that I appreciate them as a friend?

CHAPTER 7

WORK AT YOUR MARRIAGE, DON'T MARRY YOUR WORK

"Harold's wife went out and became another man's mistress
because Harold had a mistress . . . his job."
—J. Allen Petersen

How would you like to be the physician who told Magic
Johnson his basketball career was over and he might also lose
the game of life? Or the ophthalmologist who informed my
dad that, due to oxygen deprivation to his eyes, he would
become totally blind and there was no hope for a cure?

A friend of mine who is an audiologist tells how difficult it is
to break the news to new parents that their tiny child will never
hear properly. He has the unwelcome task of informing these parents that their mythical hope for a perfect child is over.

Negative news. I never get used to being the recipient or the
giver of it. But both the willingness to hear it and to relate it are a
part of living honestly and facing reality. Let me remind you of two

Washington realities that you may not want to hear. They are true but may not be easy to swallow:

1. When you are gone you might miss Washington, but Washington will not miss you. This place will not skip a beat when you are gone.

2. The ripple of your absence will be significantly felt in only one place . . . your home.

That is it. Period. Ironically, Washington is full of people who live with the illusion that their family can get along without them but the nation can't. Their children won't miss them, but Congress and the Kiwanis Club will. Their spouse can be neglected but not their seat or some speaking engagement. People who buy into this fallacy marry their work and forget to work at their marriage.

Let me say again that Washington will not skip a beat when you are gone. This community does not seriously mourn or miss anyone. Hard to believe? Let's see if an imaginary conversation about former members will bring the point home.

"When was the last time you heard anyone say anything about any former members being genuinely missed? For instance, when was the last time you heard anyone say he missed Larkin Smith, the freshman Republican who died in a plane crash?

"What's that? Oh, because he was only a freshman and a Republican in the House he is not a good example? Okay, what about Mickey Leland, the experienced Democrat who died in another plane crash right after Larkin Smith? When was the last time you heard anyone lament his absence? You say that he was not senior enough? Okay, when was the last time you heard anyone in grief over the void left by Claude Pepper? He was a true heavyweight on the Hill.

"While you think that over, let me tell you a story about one member's grief over the loss of Chairman Claude Pepper. I was sitting only seventy-five feet away from his casket having a conversation with another Democratic member. I asked him to take a minute and join me in paying my respects to this one-time leader in the House. His response startled me. He replied that he had spent enough time with the Chairman when he was alive, and he would just wait for me and then we could resume our conversation. Talk about minimal grief!

"When was the last time you heard anyone mention how much they missed Tony Coehlo, Bill Gray, Jim Wright, or Tip O'Neill? What's that? You say we should consider the other side of the Hill? Okay, when was the last time you heard anyone mention how much they and this city miss Senators Bayh, Church, or Jackson? What's that? You say these are too far back? How about Zorinsky? Still too far back? How about Hart or Heinz? How about considering groups of members? Who looks back with regret when over 25 percent of the members in the House don't return with a new session in Congress? What's that? You get the drift of what I am saying? Good. I don't like to be this blunt and I am glad to stop."

No one in this city is a vital and irreplaceable player. To believe otherwise is to believe an illusion. Veteran members of this community understand this. Experience has taught them that this community only pays serious attention to the *present* players. To be anything else is to be a non-player.

Here's what some of these veterans had to say about members and their impact on the city:

"You must understand that your departure from Congress—no matter how or why you leave—is an opportunity for others. It is good news for them. Someone will take your seat, another will take your committee assignments, and another will gladly take your office . . . if the location is good."

"I have been to members' funerals where the main topic of conversation, while we stood around the casket, was who will get the member's seat. And the body wasn't even cold yet!"

"The next time a member dies, read the papers and count the number of paragraphs written about them before it turns to the one thing political people most want to know . . . who will take their seat? It usually takes only two or three paragraphs to reach this 'important' information."

"My husband served in Congress for eight years. After his defeat in November, he went into the Sergeant at Arms office for something. His term had not yet expired, but he was forced to wait while a new member of Congress, who had not even been sworn in yet, was taken ahead of him. The message was clear: You are no longer in power."

I realize that my relaying these observations could have the opposite of the intended effect. Those who consciously or unconsciously find these incidents threatening may get angry at my premise, retreat into denial, or cling even more desperately to their work as their only source of identity, significance, and satisfaction. Obviously, that is not my goal. My desire is to inject a little realism into the political world.

I have seen too many individuals duped by the histrionic affections they receive as temporary players on the political stage. Naively trusting this new-found love, respect, and admiration, they lose interest in the one offer of love that is real and lasting—their family's.

The individuals whom I have seen enter and exit Washington with the greatest ease are those that never took themselves or this place too seriously. They came here, honored to do their best in a job that is important. They didn't become infatuated with this place. They didn't lose all balance in their lives. They remembered who they were and who they were not. They valued their primary relationships and protected them. Interestingly enough, these individuals are also the ones who appear to be the most respected and missed by their peers in Washington.

I like the attitude of the former Cabinet secretary who, when observing that his assistant secretaries were overly impressed with themselves or their titles, gently told them: "This city does not long remember Cabinet secretaries. What makes you think it will remember you?" This man served in two Cabinet posts with enormous skill, integrity, and character. While doing this he avoided the seduction of the political culture. He worked at his marriage and never married his work. In the end he excelled in both. His was a "win-win" combination.

Why don't we hear stories like this more often? Why do people get so caught up in their jobs that other important areas of life are neglected? Why do some people lose all balance in their lives? Let's explore a few reasons that have frequently been shared with me by those in political life.

If I Don't Work This Hard I Might Lose My Job

Some individuals devote their lives to their work out of one driving emotion: fear. They tell themselves, "If I don't give 110 percent of my effort, energy, and focus to my job, I will lose it." Whether it is warranted or not, this anxiety provokes a desperate attempt to do whatever is necessary to retain one's position.

It is a lousy way to live.

New members are most susceptible to this chronic state of anxiety and the frenetic lifestyle that it breeds. Afraid to upset anyone, they say yes to more than is possible and to far more than is necessary. They attempt to see as many visiting constituents as they can, speak to all visiting groups, and accept as many speaking engagements in their district as possible. In an effort to make a good impression on their party leadership and in their committees, they overextend themselves in party involvement as well.

Insecure members assume that the only requests for time, attention, and recognition that are safe for them to decline are those from their family. It is an erroneous and dangerous assumption.

More secure members learn to allocate their time more effectively. They don't live with the chronic anxiety of upsetting someone. Boundaries of self-care protect their personal lives. They learn to say no to many of the countless requests and opportunities that come their way.

As a matter of survival, most members have their staffs write computer-generated letters that are their standard response to requests for their presence at some event. Their response letters usually look something like this:

Thank you very much for your kind invitation to
_____. Due to my busy Congressional sched-
ule, I regret that I am unable to participate in your
event. If there is anything I can do for you in the future,
please do not hesitate to contact me.

Sincerely,

Member of Congress

Recently I sent personal invitations to a group of members
and their spouses for a weekend away designed specifically *for*
them as individuals and as couples. Knowing how Congressional
offices work, I closed my letters with this statement, "If you are
going to have your staff send me one of your computer-generated
garbage letters that start with, 'Thank you very much for your
kind invitation, but due to my busy Congressional schedule I
regret that I will be unable to attend,' please have them enclose a
barf bag along with their letter." A number of members called to
kid me about having been around the Hill too long and knowing
them too well.

But do you know who often receives these canned responses?
The member's family. They are the ones who, for all practical pur-
poses, hear the response that implies, "Thank you very much for
your kind invitation to (our anniversary dinner, a family member's
birthday dinner, a graduation, a prom night, an awards banquet
for a child, a school function, a sporting event, a family night, etc.),
but due to my busy Congressional schedule I regret that . . ." Is it
any wonder that some family members also need a barf bag?

Insecure members send mass mailings of these letters to their
families. Over time, either the member wakes up or the family

gives up and stops expecting the member to participate in the family. They expect less and request less. They learn to live as single-parent families. If the pattern is not resolved, eventually many *become* single-parent families through divorce.

Some things in life are far worse than losing a job.

I Prefer the Bubble of Capitol Hill to the Reality of Home

Deep-sea scuba diving has always fascinated me. When scuba divers have been in deep water, they must monitor how quickly they rise to the surface of the water. If they don't pace themselves properly, they will experience excruciating pain and possibly die from the formation of nitrogen in the blood. It is commonly called the bends.

Divers are in danger of having the bends when they are returning to the surface of the water, when they return to their natural environment. Experienced divers know that the transition between these two radically different environments must be carefully controlled or the consequences can be fatal.

This same phenomenon occurs when people transition between work and home—two completely different environments. Many individuals experience severe discomfort upon arriving home. I call it "the relational bends." Because they don't anticipate this reaction, some assume that home is a toxic and painful environment to which they cannot adapt and they begin to spend more time at work.

And, indeed, they experience less pain at work. Submersion in work seems more pleasant and less threatening than returning to what should be a normal environment for them. Being at work feels more like home. And going home feels like work.

Members of Congress—especially senators—are particularly susceptible to severe cases of the relational bends. Their work and home environments are so completely different that they need to take special care in moving from one to the other. Unless they do, they will erroneously conclude that they can only thrive in one environment, their work. They develop addictions to work and aversions to home—all because they don't understand the distinct nature of these environments and the necessary methods of transition between them.

The member's work environment is fascinating. But it is anything but natural. Once this environment is understood it becomes clear why some individuals have difficulty making the transition back to home life: They experience culture shock.

A senator gave me a helpful picture of life on the Hill. He mentioned that when he is off the Hill, but not in his home state, he is anonymous and treated like anyone else, but when his vehicle reaches Capitol Hill, he enters a bubble. Once inside this bubble everything changes. It is another world. A twilight zone. In this world everything revolves around the members. Suddenly, for them, traffic is halted, pedestrians are held back, elevators held open, and subways stopped.

Members are surrounded by a cadre of people who are paid to serve them, affirm them, and implement their ideas. All day long staff, interns, and pages are available to members. They show respect and are quick to respond to the thoughts, needs, or whims of the member. They appear excited about serving the member and have plenty of energy and time to expend. They are enthusiastic about the member, acquiesce to the member, and go out of their way to affirm the member. They spend inordinate amounts of time trying to make the member look and feel good.

In the bubble negative information is minimized and positive news is maximized. Few ever confront or contradict members. Everyone consistently appears admiring and amiable, helpful and happy. No one mentions being angry, hurt, tired, or uninterested. Like a patriot missile technician, the staff stand alert, ready to shoot down any incoming political or personal scud missile attack that may hurt, harm, or upset the member.

The senator who used this analogy and his colleagues that have confirmed it did not mean to infer that life as a member is painless. It can be a brutal lifestyle. Especially of late. But the brutality of public life, along with the normal realities of life, are remarkably assuaged when one spends extended time in the bubble.

It is not difficult to see why some individuals get a severe case of the relational bends when they leave this work environment and return home. The attitudes and responses of family members contrast drastically from those of the paid Hill employees. For many members the Hill is, quite simply, more fun, more rewarding, and less taxing. As the lite beer commercials claim, it is less filling and tastes great.

The following chart compares and contrasts these two environments. It might further clarify why some individuals have difficulty making the transition between work and home.

No wonder many members have decompression problems in the transition between these two environments. Every day when they leave Capitol Hill, they encounter a mini-Copernican Revolution. Does the world revolve around them or others? After being the center of attention all day, some individuals have problems admitting the universe does not revolve around them. Indeed, by day, in their work place, the world does revolve around them. But by night, in their home, the world revolves around others.

At Work

1. Treated like a "hero."
2. A world of fantasy.
3. Staff exists to meet my needs.
4. Treated like "Superman."
5. Deal with national family issues.
6. Deal with banking and saving and loan crisis.
7. Deal with catastrophic health insurance.
8. People eagerly listen to me.
9. People are sensitive to my needs.
10. The world revolves around me.
11. Expected to help change the world.

At Home

1. Treated like an "ordinary" person.
2. A world of reality.
3. Spouse expects me to meet his/her needs.
4. Treated like Clark Kent.
5. Deal with *my* family issues.
6. Deal with *our* budget crisis.
7. Deal with minor catastrophes of our family life.
8. People expect me to listen eagerly to them.
9. People expect me to be sensitive to their needs.
10. The world revolves around others.
11. Expected to change light bulbs, diapers, etc.

The most healthy and insightful members adapt to the constant transition between these two very different worlds. Those who are maladaptive relegate their lives to be lived primarily in the work environment. They spend only minimal and token time in the seemingly more difficult place called home. Over time they learn to love their work. It is much easier than working at love.

Maybe the Senate wife was correct when she told me, "The reason that the Senate stays in so late at night is because the senators don't want to go home."

One member, after reflecting upon the vastly different experience of the bubble versus the home, commented: "It is very difficult for members to handle the dichotomy of the Hill and home life. After being treated as an extraordinary person all day, it is difficult to go home and be treated as an ordinary person. It is easy to think, 'Who are you to question my judgment when no one else has questioned my judgment all day long?' "

All of us who spend a large amount of time on Capitol Hill often experience culture shock when returning home. Two recent days stand out for me.

The first began with an early breakfast at a downtown club. I met with an individual preparing to give a series of seminars to several groups of members. He wanted my insight on understanding the culture of Capitol Hill. After this breakfast I spent a full hour with a senator who had asked me to meet with him. From there I spent individual time with one of the most respected members in the House. Following that meeting, I chaired a ninety-minute discussion with three other members of Congress. Next I scurried to the White House where I had been invited to have lunch. After lunch I went to my counseling office and met with two clients for individual therapy. Only then did I return home . . . back to reality.

When I walked in the door my kids didn't care about what I had done or with whom I had met that day. Only one thing mattered to them: Could we have a family floor night? Later as I was tossing my kids in the air and then lying on the floor while they climbed all over me, I remember thinking, "This is the most important thing I have done today."

The other day involved the same clash between these two worlds. I had met with members all day. My last meeting was a dynamic and stimulating discussion with five senators that lasted one hour. After our meeting I raced home to get in a quick workout before slipping out for the evening to see some clients. After putting on my jogging clothes, I went outside and my daughters were playing hide-and-seek with one of their friends. Again, they had wanted to know only one thing: Would I play with them? I wanted to say no. But I chose, reluctantly at first, to say yes. So, I covered my eyes, counted out loud to fifty, and shouted "ready or not here I come."

When it was my turn to hide, I ran around the yard, hiding once by climbing a pine tree, another time by trying to make my two-hundred-pound frame inconspicuous under the cushion of a deck chair, and lastly I lay as flat as possible in the grass behind a Blue Spruce tree. Once again I couldn't help but think, "One hour ago I was dressed in a suit and sitting with five United States senators. Now here I am lying on the ground playing hide-and-seek. And this is the most important thing I will do today."

Playing hide-and-seek reminded me of how good it was to feel like a kid again, to laugh with glee, to know the joy of relationships. Playing with my daughters and their friend was far more satisfying, significant, and fulfilling than teaching a group of senators in the Capitol would ever be.

My Life Is Derived from My Work

Some people marry their work and forget to work at their marriage for a third reason: They believe their worth is derived from their work. This conclusion is not always consciously decided; it evolves over time from some questionable premises, such as:

My esteem comes from my employment.

My worth comes from my work.

My person is defined by my profession.

My significance as a human being is defined by my stardom at work.

Nothing is wrong with these beliefs if they are held loosely. If these premises are viewed as *part* of the person's life or as just one aspect of the composite picture, it is fine. If they are viewed as one piece of the puzzle that reflects the individual, they are harmless.

The danger arises when someone defines their worth, significance, and value only by their work and title. These people cannot separate themselves from their work. They are workaholics, not from a strong dedication to their work, but from being hooked on the narcotic of achievement-based esteem.

It is *extremely difficult* to uproot this belief.

When people derive their sense of value almost exclusively from their job or their title, their job begins to meet (and cover up) some of their deepest needs for significance. Their worth has become inextricably welded to their work. Their identity is fused to their profession and they will risk nothing that might seriously jeopardize their position. To do so would endanger their own sense of self.

On a recent Sunday my family and I went to an open house for a new business fifty miles from Washington. The event had nothing to do with Washington or politics, and no one seemed interested in meeting any Washingtonians. But I noticed a former senator who had also been the chairman of a key Senate committee.

As we walked past him, I heard him introduce himself to everyone by saying, "Hello, I'm former Senator . . ." I thought to myself, "No one needs to know who he is, but he has a need to tell everyone who he is—or more accurately, who he used to be."

I always feel compassion for former members who fused their worth to their title as senator, congressman, congresswoman, speaker, leader, etc. Their sense of value is rooted in who they used to be and what they used to do. Their worth remains linked to their past, which diminishes their ability to enjoy their present lives. Their glory has faded, and they try to shore it up by not allowing others to forget their past accomplishments.

Another incident illustrates this. I drove to a Virginia office building to meet a friend for lunch. I wound my way into the underground parking garage and paid the attendant. From there I headed toward the parking area. No reserved parking existed so I was able to park anywhere in the entire garage. That is, anywhere except one particular slot. As people drove into the garage, one sign was prominently displayed so that you could not avoid seeing it as you drove in: "Reserved for the Honorable . . ." It was a former member who had spent over two decades in Congress and was now in the private sector. His security or significance hung from the sign that bore his title from former days. He needed people to know that he used to be a player and a star on Capitol Hill.

One final illustration of this occurred in the fall of 1978 when I was new to Capitol Hill and naive about the culture. Several days after the November election as I rode in an elevator in the Cannon building, an older man got on and I simply said hello and asked him how his day was going. I had no idea who he was and I only addressed him because I like people and he was a fellow human being. As we rode in the elevator and then talked in the hall, he mentioned that he was not doing well. He was despondent. He was glad to talk to me even though I was nothing more than a caring stranger. He was one of the old bulls in the Congress, and he had just been fatally gored. He'd lost his election. But in his mind he had lost much more than his seat. He'd lost his identity, his purpose, and his sense of significance. Over the years his value as a person had become entangled in his work and title. When he lost his seat, he lost it all.

Most individuals who are caught in this web that entangles work and worth agree at a cerebral level that they should keep their life more balanced. They give intellectual assent to the importance of time invested in primary relationships. But in the end they struggle with actually acting upon their acknowledgment because spending time with family does not appear to satisfy. So while giving assent to the importance of relationships, they give their time and energy to their vocation.

This is why some members occasionally change their positions on votes that might contradict their deepest held beliefs or values. If holding a position creates so much heat that it could cause their career to crash, they will jettison their position to save their career. Naturally, their rationale for their new-found frame of reference sounds legitimate. They will put a favorable political spin on it.

Psychologically, they are protecting their career at all costs because losing their seat is not simply losing their job. It means much more. It means they lose their sense of self, significance, and worth. Character goes out the window in order to keep their career aloft. For them massive cognitive dissonance is more bearable than a career that is in disarray.

But this wasn't the case with Mac, a member who had retired early after six terms in the House. When I asked him why he told me that he could no longer live with himself while playing to the media. He said, "For years I have been casting votes that I don't believe. I did not have the courage to do what I believed was right. But I could no longer live with my duplicity. So I quit. And I am glad to be gone."

Here was one individual whose commitment to character, at least in the end, was stronger than his commitment to his career. He successfully avoided merging his worth to his job. As a result he was free to walk away from the Hill.

Is he a dying breed? I hope not.[1]

Unquestionably, serving in the United States Congress is an honor. And it is a task that deserves excellence. But it is possible to do one's work with excellence and still keep balance and perspective in one's personal life. To do this an individual must resist the allure of Washington by facing the reality of this city. It will not miss us when we are gone. The only place where our absence will be significantly felt, and where we honestly cannot be replaced, is in our home. Period.

Note

1. Let me introduce a thought worth further research. Why are people zealots for causes? Certainly some causes merit zeal. But psychologically, many people are zealots for causes *due to the causes' benefits for them*. The cause they embrace gives them a sense of self, a purpose, a place to feel like a player. These people are deeply committed to their cause because it is meeting their deepest needs. They are even willing to risk their lives for this cause because to separate them from the cause is to take their life from them anyway. Without it they would feel like a zero—having no worth, purpose, or significance.

Think about It

The following questions are for your personal reflection. You may reflect on them alone or discuss them with your spouse, children, or a group of your peers.

1. Do I agree with the notion that Washington does not miss people after they are gone?

2. Do I secretly hope that my impact and role will be so great that I will break the norm and be profoundly missed by this city?

3. "The only place the ripple of your absence will be significantly felt is in your home." Do I agree or disagree with this thought? Why?

4. Is the ripple of my absence being felt in my home? Where? By whom? What do they need from me? What do I want to do about it?

5. Is there a "bubble phenomena" in my work world? Have I learned to prefer this world of preferential treatment to the world of reality in my home?

6. Do I get "the bends" when I return home? Do I think this is a normal transition or just a struggle to avoid?

7. Have I welded my sense of worth to my work? Would I be able to leave my work without threatening my sense of self? Why do I keep doing my job? What personal or psychological needs of mine does it meet?

8. Am I trying so hard to meet my own needs that I cannot focus on the needs of my family? Have I married my work and forgotten to work at my marriage?

CHAPTER 8

MANAGE YOUR SCHEDULE TO MANAGE YOUR LIFE

"Eighty percent of life is just showing up."
—Woody Allen

They had the banter down pat. Each of them knew their lines and could be trusted to come in right on cue. This night was no exception. The father and son team began to work the crowd as always. They stood in their backyard greeting the guests who had turned out at the fund-raiser for the father's re-election. Everything was rolling smoothly, until someone asked the young boy while he was standing next to his congressman father, "What do you want to be when you grow up?"

It was a standard question. And the young buck had a standard response. Looking the person straight in the eye (as many Congressional children are taught) he was expected to say with pride, "When I grow up I want to be a fireman, a dad, and a congressman!"

This response always brought warm laughs and nods of approval.

But this particular night he blew his lines. When asked the familiar question he looked at the individual and responded, "When I grow up I want to be a fireman and a dad." His dad waited for his son to finish his lines, but the son said nothing more. So the father prodded him, "Go on, Son, tell him the rest. Tell him that you want to be a congressman when you grow up." This time the child looked his dad in the eye and said, "I don't want to be a congressman when I grow up. Because you can't be a congressman and a dad at the same time."

Can you guess whether this little boy felt like a priority or a prop in his father's life? I hurt every time I reflect on it. Can this pain be avoided in other political families? Yes, I believe it is possible to be a successful spouse, parent, and member simultaneously. But it is not an easy balancing act.

Those who have successfully managed to win in their public and private lives have one thing in common: They learned to manage their schedules. They are not the victims of their schedules. Planning your schedule requires clear focus, courage, and commitment. Without these you are dead in the water.

Hitting the Bull's-Eye

As an archer I understand the need to focus. When an archer stands ninety feet away from a target, a vast difference exists between hoping to hit the bull's-eye versus carefully concentrating on a specific spot no larger than a quarter.

Most people want to hit bull's-eyes on three targets: work, marriage, and parenting. Hitting one out of three will not do. But success is rarely accidental. To score well you need to focus *carefully* on each bull's-eye. You must choose and determine what you will aim for or you'll forget to aim at all of the targets.

For example, when I want to stay in shape as an archer, I try to shoot fifty arrows each day. But it would do me little good to shoot forty arrows at one target, seven at a second, and three at a third. If I want to hit all three targets I must be balanced in the number of shots I take at each of them. I've found it's much easier to do in archery than it is in life!

In order to decide what to focus on, we must confront our values. If we recognize and know our values, it is much easier to schedule our time. For example, if we decide that our schedule will reflect our values, we can more readily ascertain when to say yes or when to say no to opportunities. If our values are not clear, our scheduling decisions will be hit or miss, especially those times when we have an abundance of choices.

Successful political families have learned to distinguish between:

—living by priorities versus living by preferences,

—doing the important versus doing the urgent,

—doing what is necessary versus doing what is desirable.

Because these families keep the important in focus, scheduling and decision-making is much easier. Their focus serves as a boundary and gives them parameters to use as a guideline. Their focus frees them to keep their lives functionally balanced most of the time.

Interestingly, most members I talk to have never clarified or written down what they hold as their ultimate focus. Even fewer have ever thought of using their definition of what is important, necessary, and top priority as a basis for scheduling decisions. But to do so is very freeing.

My wife and I enjoy speaking and traveling. In recent years we have had numerous requests to speak in China, Western Europe, Africa, Latin America, the Soviet Union (before its collapse), and, recently, Russia. Guess how many of these invitations we have accepted? Zero. Why? Our priorities determine our schedule. While our children are young, we choose to limit our time away from them. Admittedly, our *preference* is to go on all these trips. But part of our focus is on our children, so we respectfully decline the offers to speak. When our children are older, our focus will change and then we will jump at these opportunities.

Establishing Boundaries

What follows are some creative and unique boundaries established by political families in order to ensure that they do what they believe is important, necessary, and top priority. Consider which of these might help you hit your targets:

1. Set aside one day a week for yourself and your family. One member who came perilously close to losing his family in his drive to become a member decided that Sunday is for himself, his family, and worship. Period. It does not matter what the event or if the president is in his district, if it is on a Sunday count him out. This boundary makes it easier for him, his family, and his staff to know the limits. It doesn't trap them. It frees them.

2. If Congress is not in session, don't attend evening receptions. Members who have established this boundary go home when they know there are no more votes. This guideline, if held with regularity, can help you maintain your health, marriage, and family.

Any member who has been around for a while knows that receptions can kill you in one of two ways: they will burn you out or they will bore you to death.

3. If your spouse isn't invited to an event, don't attend. A cabinet secretary had this simple rule. No exceptions. Is it any wonder that their marriage thrived in the middle of their political life?

4. Eat breakfast with your family every weekday. A senator I know did this for the last ten years he was in the Senate. When the Senate was in session most of the night—even if he got home at 5:00 A.M.—he would set his alarm and get up with his family. Then he would return to bed for a brief nap when his kids went to school.

He used this time to give each person the spotlight. He would ask what was on their hearts and minds that day. Afterward his family briefly prayed for each other before going their separate ways. I would guess that his children left for school with more than just breakfast. Each day they left feeling safe, loved, and valued. Not a bad way to unwrap a new day.

5. Attend as many of your children's school events as possible. This is not easy. The member who gave me this guideline told how sometimes things were quite frantic as he and his wife would leave a soccer game and then change into their formal evening clothes while in the car. But they kept a terrific sense of humor and sustained their love for each other. This family hit three bull's-eyes . . . marriage, family, and career.

6. Together with your spouse decide each of the important and non-negotiable family events in the upcoming year. This list could include anniversaries, children and grandchildren's birthdays, graduations, recitals, etc. Then, give this schedule to your staff so that political events can be scheduled around your family planning.

This ensures your family receives prime time rather than leftover scraps. It is much healthier for everyone.

7. Establish clear limits regarding the number of weekends you will travel to the district each month. For some it is every third weekend. For others it is once a month or every other weekend. The safety of their seats and the stages of their family lives are all factored into this decision.

Beware of the temptation to return every weekend while your family stays in Washington. No family can hold their breath that long. Interestingly, the members who return to their district every weekend while their family remains in Washington often lose their seat—and everything else. They don't hit any bull's-eye.

One member told me he reserves all day Monday to work in his district. His constituents gladly adjust their events to accommodate his schedule. On Sunday evening he flies back to his district. Then he is scheduled Monday from 6:00 A.M. until late evening with events in his district. After this he returns to Washington late in the evening or early Tuesday morning. This allows him to work effectively in his district while having the bulk of the weekend to get refreshed and have time with his family. He hits all three targets.

The creativity and commitment of the families who live by these guidelines give hope that marriages and families can thrive in the political world. But it's not easy.

The Stuff of Courage and Commitment

No question about it. It takes guts to make the tough calls when ordering and scheduling a political life. Oftentimes a person will take more flack for making the right call than they will for a poor one. When members focus exclusively on their political lives and work, they rarely receive any criticism from constituents, colleagues, or staffs. But if they start to make scheduling decisions based on keeping their priorities straight, all of these groups may question what the member is doing.

People on the Hill believe there is *nothing* more important for members than protecting their seats . . . no matter what the cost. It is a debatable premise. If you doubt this, talk to those members who have won their seats and lost a son or spouse. Ask someone who kept his district but lost his daughter. Learn from them. Become wise from their mistakes and thereby avoid some of your own.

Learn also from the people who were committed and courageous enough to put their families first. Listen to one family's inspiring story.

Every time the phone rang that day Susie told her mother, "That's Daddy! He's calling to tell me he is not coming to my awards banquet tonight. I know that's Daddy." It was a big day in her life. It meant a lot to her and Susie wanted her dad to come and be a part of it. She wanted him to stop, step out of his world, and get into her mud puddle. That evening Langley High School was holding its annual athletic banquet, and she was receiving an award for her participation in sports. After spending years watching her parents honored, she wanted them to watch her honored by others. She wanted the spotlight.

But it was also a big night in her father's political life. It was an election year and the biggest political event of the year for his state was occurring that evening. It was *the* event. And it was in the principal city in his district. Bush, the vice president at the time, was having a major fund raiser for his presidential campaign. All of the key people in the state's Republican party would be in attendance.

Word got out that this member was not sure if he was going to attend this election event. Naturally, Bush and his people wanted this member present and visible to help create the appearance of strong statewide support. To sweeten the pie, the White House called and asked the member to fly to the event with the V.P. on his plane. It was an enticing trump card to play.

The member wrestled with his decision. What should he focus on? What should his priorities be? Meanwhile, his daughter wrestled with her fear and hope. Fear that her dad would not show up. Hope that he would.

As both events began, Susie searched the audience. She was looking for the one face, the one guest, that she desperately wanted there along with her mother. Without his presence, her honor would feel empty and hollow. With him, it would be a rich memory. Finally, her face brightened and her heart soared. Dad had just walked in! Bull's-eye.

A Very Different Message

Unfortunately, Susie's dad isn't typical. Most of the stories I hear end much differently. For instance the story about the father who received a call that an important vote had come up. It was the day of his son's wedding, but this father decided that it was more important for him to vote than to see his son get married. So, he left the wedding and went to Washington to cast his vote.

Or the story a prominent Washingtonian mother told me about her son: It was the young boy's birthday, and she was having a birthday party for him. As his friends began arriving, one of the kids asked the boy why his father was not at his birthday party. The son responded, "My father has more important things to do than come to my birthday party."

Let me be blunt. I think these fathers are both fools. These parents are aiming at the wrong target. Both missed very significant days in their sons' lives. While they will most likely forget the reasons for their absences, their sons may some day remember one thing: Dad loved his job more than he loved me.

I repeatedly hear children and adults reflect on their earlier years and grieve that their mom and dad "had more important things to do than attend my . . ." Their hearts ache with the loss that they have never felt cherished, focused upon, or viewed as a priority by their parents. As they process their pain they begin to wonder, "What were my parents doing that they did not have time for me? Was the work of my parents really that important? Maybe I am unimportant and not worthy of being valued and viewed as a priority. All I know is that I have to interpret my parents' schedules as a reflection of their values and their commitment (or lack of commitment) to me. And it hurts."

When I hear about members who miss significant events in the lives of their spouses and children because of something more important to do on Capitol Hill, I can't help but wonder about their motives. Could it be that the members who miss family events cannot handle someone else, even their own children, in the spotlight? Could it be that it is a way for the member to make a statement about how important and needed he is in Washington? Is it a need to create the illusion that the country really cannot function without him? As a senator told me, "There is no bigger ego trip than to be in your state and then be called back to Washington on urgent national business." Could it be that members like this are so preoccupied with their own ego gratification that they cannot take time to honor others . . . even their own families?

Pay Attention at Mission Control

Our schedules—not our words—reflect our beliefs. William Raspberry, a *Washington Post* writer, in his typically courageous and cogent way, reminds us of our continual need to focus on our marriage and family. He writes:

> Marriage isn't primarily about individual men and women. Marriage is about *families*. It has developed over the millennia as the best way of raising healthy, competent children—in short, as the naturally selected arrangement for perpetuating the human species.
>
> Obviously there can be other arrangements. There *are* other arrangements, including single-parent households, no parent households, communes and kibbutzim. But mostly these are alternative arrangements triggered by special circumstances. The universal preference, over both time and geography, has been for the family headed by husband and wife.
>
> It's possible to argue that the crumbling of the marriage institution has left individual men and women no worse off—perhaps even better off—than when they were locked into unhappy and unfulfilling marriages. But it's hard to make the case that *children* are not worse off.
>
> Whether the measure is teen pregnancy or teen violence, adolescent rootlessness or adolescent suicide, the indications are that our children are less happy, less healthy and less secure than we were and that things aren't getting better.
>
> And they won't get better, I fear, until we learn once

again to honor, preserve and strengthen the one arrangement that seems to offer the best chance for producing healthy, happy and competent children: the child-centered marriage.[1]

We need a child-centered schedule if we are to produce children who are healthy, happy, and competent. It will not happen accidentally or on the backstroke. It is the result of intention.

Let me share a simple picture of parenting that helps my wife and me stay on task in our parenting. Maybe it will help you.

We view our children as two separate rockets. Each of them sits on a launch pad preparing for blast off into their own individual orbit—adulthood. It will take approximately two decades of our best effort to prepare each rocket for takeoff. We believe this is the most important venture of our lives. If we succeed, our children and the next generation benefit from the successful launch of two rockets.

As we prepare to launch our rockets, we pay careful attention to two principal components: the fuel system and the guidance system. One system provides power. The other provides direction. If both of these are not working properly, it's not likely that the rocket will be successfully launched and able to sustain a stable orbit.

A child's emotional tank is like the fuel system. The proper amount and mixture of emotional fuel (i.e. love, focused attention, affection, affirmation, etc.) is vital to their future adult lives. When mixed correctly it helps to ensure a successful launch into independence. It also determines an individual's ability to engage in healthy and intimate relationships as an adult. If a person's emotional fuel tank is insufficiently full or poorly mixed, they may flounder for years. Instead of soaring, this rocket will spend years trying to fill or repair its fuel tank.

The guidance system of a rocket is equally important. The computers and gyroscope provide direction and stability. Its component parts consist of things called values, beliefs, morals, and convictions. Without a guidance system the rocket can recklessly careen in space doing incalculable damage to itself and other rockets.

Today, many scholars and parents believe that parents should put only minimal guidance systems into the rockets they are launching. They have bought the notion that too much interference will somehow inhibit a child's orbit in the adult world. They naively assume that this will restrict the creative flight path of the individual.

This notion appeals to busy parents for two reasons: It requires much less time and energy on their part, and most parents don't have a clue about how to install a guidance system in their child because their own system is barely functional.

Without a guidance system the rocket is out-of-control. It is a chaotic and terrifying ride causing extensive damage to themselves and others.

Many too-busy parents are casually launching rockets into space. As the rockets are about to be launched, there is all the anticipation of the *Challenger* astronauts. And too often the results are identical. The rocket blows up at takeoff.

Parents, pay attention at mission control. You are more needed at home than you are on the Hill. I frequently tell members "I don't want your kids as my clients." They don't need the pain and I don't need the business. I have enough business to last me a lifetime. The world already has too many rockets with fuel tanks and guidance systems that are malfunctioning.

To ensure that we function well in our careers, marriages, and family, we need to assume responsibility for our schedules.

Who Sets the Schedule?

Remember the assassination attempt of President Reagan and the confusion about "who is in charge here?" That same role confusion often occurs in political offices. No one is really clear about who is officially in charge. Usually, staff members assume as much authority in this area as is allowed by the member. Many members yield so much authority to their staffs that they are no longer served and counseled by them; they are controlled by them. When this happens the member's schedule has one priority: political life. Marriage and family life are little more than an afterthought for the staff. In fact, the staff often resents them and at best tolerates them.

I have heard members angry with themselves and their staffs for allowing them to become outrageously over-booked. It is not uncommon to hear, "I don't even have time to go to the bathroom." Members can avoid this by clearly communicating their goals to their staffs. The staff will watch and test the member to see if these are values/beliefs that are lived out or whether they are simply ideals that are espoused. They respect and honor the former (although repeatedly test them to see if they still hold). They ignore the latter.

On the other extreme are members who are enamored with their right to be served. They treat their staffs as if nothing is as fulfilling or important in their lives as staying at work. They expect them always to be available—even when at home—in case they are needed. Their staffs are expected to aim at only one target—work—and to ignore their primary relationships.

I encourage members to determine and manage their schedules aggressively for two reasons. The first is from my own experience. I have lived life on the edge and at full speed. I know what it is like when I let my schedule get out of control for extended periods of time. And I know the result. The quality and joy of my marriage and family life are directly impacted.

Secondly, I have seen too many political families die of neglect. These families had all the basic ingredients for a strong and satisfying family life. But the members were so busy chasing the Holy Grail of their careers that they lost their balance and focus in life. They were so busy aiming at the target of their careers they never even noticed the targets of marriage and family had fallen down or disappeared. When they do finally notice, it is often too late. And they are staggered at the hollow victory of hitting one bull's-eye while missing two other targets.

If members want to balance their lives, they need to set clear limits with their staffs. Many members work in public service because they enjoy people. They like to keep people and relationships "happy." They like to be liked. However, their desire to be liked can make it difficult for them to establish boundaries. They struggle with setting limits, saying no, and honestly expressing their needs. They are *too* nice. These individuals need to learn that they—not their staffs—are in charge of their time and lives. Members are not dolls which are wound up by the staff and then pointed in the direction the staff desires for them to go. They have to take personal responsibility for the management of their schedules and lives. When members don't take charge, their staffs overbook them so much that the members—or the families—are pushed to the edge of physical or emotional exhaustion.

Over scheduling happens partly because many staff members confuse busyness with significance. They believe they are helping the member by keeping him as busy as possible. Members often forget that many of their staffs are desperately trying to impress or please them. In order to show their boss how vital they are many staff members look for ways to get the member key publicity, interviews, speaking engagements, fund-raising events, etc. What few are willing to see is that when they are too successful, the result is a hectic schedule which prevents a healthy balance and pace of life for the very people they are trying to help. Fully-booked schedules cut into the limited amount of time members have to allot in the multiple areas of their lives.

Another reason members' schedules get out of control is that some members develop a co-dependent relationship with their staffs that disempowers them. Many members give more and more control of their schedules, and their lives, to their staffs. Over time these members can grow so accustomed to the staff telling them where to go, what to do, what to say, etc. that they lose their own sense of autonomy. Both the member and the staff believe the other is needed to survive.

It is amazing to see how distressed some staff members become if there is a schedule change they need to tell the member about. Or how concerned they are if a member's flight is changed or canceled. They worry if the member will know what to do or be able to handle the change. They stop treating the member as a well-functioning adult and treat the member like a little child. The few members who get hooked into this pattern of relating, do not mature or become more capable and competent. They regress and become more dependent on their staffs to take care of the most basic aspects of their lives.

When I was a little boy growing up in the cold Chicago winters, my mother would often send me to school in a snowsuit with notes pinned to my jacket. I often kid the members, saying this is how they strike me when they have given too much control of their lives and schedules to their staffs. Their lives are reduced to schedule cards from staff members dictating where they should go and what to do when they get there.

Members, when you give too much control to your staffs, your lives will most likely get out of control. Remember, the pacing and expenditure of your daily lives is your responsibility.

* * *

In closing let me say that determining core values and beliefs can be difficult and frightening. It can be a revelation. Some people discover they are so busy saying yes to the requests and needs of others that they are forced to say no to their own needs or the needs of their families. This selflessness, when taken to the extreme, is self-abuse. It will burn out the individual and make them sick or bitter over time.

On the other end of the spectrum are those who discover they are miles away from self-abuse. They have been saying no to others (and often their primary relationships) and saying yes to themselves. They have been living selfishly. Indulgently. Despite all their rhetoric, they have been living for themselves. Period. What they tell themselves is appropriate self-care, is, in actuality, blatant selfishness. Under the guise of "responsibility as a member," they rationalize a lifestyle dictated by their desires and preferences and avoid the reality of their primary tasks. What makes the Washington political community so unique is that it attracts people who live at both extremes.

But individuals who are honest with themselves and others

about their motives and who take time to determine their beliefs and values have a much clearer focus. They know what targets they want to shoot for in their lives. Knowing this, they can let their schedules be a reflection of these values. Members who do not do this set themselves or their spouses up as a different kind of candidate . . . the perfect candidate for an affair. We will explore how this occurs in the next chapter.

Note

1. William Raspberry, "Rescuing marriage before it's too late," *Washington Post*, 3 January 1992, A23.

Think about It

The following questions are for your personal reflection. You may reflect on them alone or discuss them with your spouse, children, or a group of your peers.

1. Have I ever clarified in writing my bottom-line beliefs and values? What are they?

2. Do I really desire to hit a bull's-eye on the targets of career, marriage, and family? If I could only aim at one or two, which would I pick?

3. Does my schedule for the last month reflect the priorities that I espouse? Why or why not?

4. At times it takes enormous courage to live out one's values. Do I have what it takes to do this? Am I the victim of my schedule or the determiner of it?

5. Some people do not know how to say no to others. Some do not know how to say no to themselves. Which side of the wagon am I inclined to fall off of?

6. What do I need to include or exclude in my schedule to keep balance in my life?

7. Is there time in my schedule for physical exercise? For fun?

CHAPTER 9

THE MAKING OF A CANDIDATE...
FOR AN AFFAIR

"There is no free lunch."

It was fall. The mating season for deer was in full swing. Like a *National Geographic* film crew, I was in the right place at the right time. I had been sitting for several hours on a tree stand deep in the woods. Twenty yards to my left two yearlings were feeding. I let them play and browse. Out of the swamp in front of me the first one came. A big eight-point buck with only one thing on his mind. He came straight toward me and then angled off eighty yards to my right into a thicket. I watched him and waited.

A few minutes later a large doe came out of the swamp and followed the same path as the buck. Only she stopped and fed fifty yards from me. I watched and waited. Moments later a seven-point buck came out of the swamp and headed toward the doe. I continued to watch and wait.

Just as the seven-point buck reached the doe, the eight-point buck returned with several does following him. When the two bucks were about fifty yards apart they saw each other—and everything broke loose. They stopped for one moment, raised their heads and racks to full height, and then they charged.

They collided at full speed and locked horns. They looked like two sumo wrestlers . . . pushing, shoving, legs spread wide for footing while trying to throw the other off balance. They never let up. They never unlocked their antlers. They never looked at the six does who were watching. And they never noticed they were fighting right toward me. They were too intense, too preoccupied, and too focused to see the big picture. So the bigger and stronger eight-point kept pushing the seven-point in my direction.

Finally, at twenty-seven yards to my right, the bucks unlocked their horns to get fresh footing and to ready themselves for another charge. It was all I needed. I raised my bow, drew it back, focused, and released the arrow. Thwack! Neither buck knew what happened. Within two seconds the seven-point buck was history and the eight-point stood there, trying to figure out what he had done that was so extraordinarily effective.

As I calmed down from the excitement of seeing a rare moment in nature, I realized I had much more than a freezer full of venison for my family. I had just witnessed a lesson about the power of passion. It can consume us, blur our perspectives, and drive us to abandon our caution and commitments.

I was reminded of the words of one politician to his son about individuals sucked into adultery. King Solomon wrote, "All at once he follows her, as an ox goes to the slaughter, or *as a stag is caught fast till an arrow pierces its entrails; . . . he does not know that it will cost him his life"* (Proverbs 7:22-23, italics mine).

Affairs. At first glance they may seem manageable, containable, and even useful. I have often heard people describe the early stages of an affair as being exciting, enticing, exhilarating, energizing, enriching, intoxicating, powerful, forceful, passionate, beyond my wildest expectation, invigorating, affirming, full of sincerity, the ultimate transparency, the love I have been waiting for all my life.

Affairs can also be described as addictive, duplicitous, a world of illusion, profoundly destructive, and deadly.

Our culture downplays and makes light of affairs. It presents them as commonplace, almost something to be expected. They are to be something that is tolerated and winked at by observers. But when you spend hours each week dealing with the fallout of an affair, you do not conclude that they are innocuous events that are "no big deal."

One of my personal friends and a leader of my community recently left his wife after thirty years of marriage. Like so many others before him, my friend did not know the warning signs or the overwhelming power of an affair. He has yet to discover that affairs are deeply destructive and have a ripple effect that is transgenerational. It is not easy to put Humpty Dumpty together again.

What is an affair? Let me give you a working definition: *An affair is an attempt to have legitimate needs met in illegitimate ways.* Please note that nothing is wrong with having legitimate needs. These are normal and appropriate. There is nothing wrong with the desire to have our legitimate needs met in appropriate ways. But in an affair people are utilizing unhealthy methods of meeting very acceptable needs.

Remember the Rolaids commercials that aired years ago? People were asked, "How do you spell relief?" They would reply "R-O-L-A-I-D-S." The underlying question that leads to most affairs is just that: "How do you spell relief?" Individuals who have affairs are attempting to figure out how to spell *relief.* Again, there is nothing wrong with that. But, when they spell relief "A-F-F-A-I-R," they are eliminated from the spelling bee. And their discomfort will not go away. It may be numbed or temporarily forgotten. But it will remain until the source is identified and dealt with in a legitimate way. Treating the discomforts of life with an extramarital liaison is bad medicine. It is one of those occasions in which the cure is worse than the disease . . . even if the medicine does seem to taste good.

Numerous types of affairs exist along with multiple reasons that give rise to them. But my purpose here isn't to give a clinical analysis of the causal factors and therapeutic strategy for treatment. Nor is my purpose to look at those individuals with major character disorders who might be predisposed to have an affair. Instead, I want to examine how Capitol Hill is a remarkably good breeding ground for the germination of affairs. We will then explore how to see them coming and how to avoid entanglement in them.

Fertile Soil for an Affair

Sometimes it appears that affairs "just happen," as if they occur by spontaneous combustion. It's true that there usually is one particular moment of combustion when the affair bursts to life. But when individuals begin to look at how their affairs develop, they usually recognize that the stage was set long before the affair occurred. It is the proverbial tinder box just waiting for the match to be lit. Political life can help build the tinder box and then provide the match to light it.

Several preconditions create an atmosphere for "an affair waiting to happen." The following are ones common for individuals on the Hill. As you look at this list, consider which of these are applicable to your life. The more you can identify with, the more cautious and aware you need to be.

A schedule that allows little time to be with your spouse. As we noted in the previous chapter, when couples slip into a lifestyle that allows them little time together, their sense of oneness erodes. They move from feeling like life companions and partners to feeling like roommates.

Initially this may not seem to matter, particularly if both are involved in work that keeps them occupied. However, over time, this schedule results in two people living parallel lives. They may be civil, cordial, and polite with each other, but they will not feel emotionally close. They begin to feel out of sync with each other. Their marriage is often reduced to toleration, accommodation, and mediocrity. Ironically, the more bland the relationship becomes, the more it is avoided. This only further fuels the isolation and the growing discontent.

Couples can live for years this way. In fact, many Washingtonians have turned this into an art form. Their marriages are unconsciously-orchestrated elegant dances. The goal of these elegant dances is to give the partners the sensation of moving together without ever having to risk real intimacy and commitment. They master moving in tandem without bumping into one another.

The danger occurs when one or both partners begin to sense a desire for something more. They want more intensity in their lives, more passion. They hunger for more than endless discussions about the logistics of coordinating schedules. They want more than insipid, forced conversation. They want more than mediocre sex. They want to be known, understood, and accepted in the core of their beings. They want, as AT&T says, to "reach out and touch someone." But they have grown so accustomed to not connecting with each other that they believe they no longer can. It seems impossible, so they barely try. Consequently, rather than working hard to cultivate connection within their marriage, they seek it outside their marriage. Suddenly their tight schedules mysteriously have room for a third party.

A mate who is starving for legitimate needs to be met. Too frequently I have sat in a member's dining room with senators and representatives who tell me their mates are involved in affairs. I care deeply about their pain and confusion. However, I eventually get around to asking them one pointed question: "Do you know it is possible to starve a mate into having an affair?" This question often takes them off guard, but begins to make sense as I explain what I mean.

Unknowingly, many members systematically starve their mates for time, tenderness, attention, affection, and intimacy. When a mate's hunger is acute, she becomes a great candidate for an affair.

There is a proverb that sheds light on this phenomenon: "He who is sated loathes honey, but to one who is hungry, everything bitter is sweet." The writer suggests that when a person is genuinely satisfied, it is much easier to resist things that are available even though they are desirable. For example, I can be an easy mark for any waiter offering me hot apple pie. But if I have just finished a good and satisfying meal, it is much easier for me to say no to a waiter's offer of dessert. I can do this because I am satisfied. On the other hand, if I am hungry I am much less selective about what I will eat. I lower my standards as my hunger increases. Severe hunger can seduce all of us into accepting foods that we would never consider under normal circumstances.

When we starve our spouses, it is possible for them to become so hungry that they settle for junk food. In the beginning this junk food doesn't taste bitter, it tastes good. To a starving person any food is better than no food.

Some members are so engrossed in their work that they never grasp the intensity of their mates' needs, even when verbalized. Some members become so self-absorbed, preoccupied, and driven that they forget to consider their own spouses seriously. Without knowing it, these members continue asking their spouses to hold their breath and tolerate the hunger pangs a little longer.

An ignored and hungry spouse becomes very vulnerable. Starving people are not particularly discriminating. Often someone comes along who makes them feel listened to, cared for, and taken seriously. These available people appear in the form of neighbors, the couple's close friends, other members, staff, or co-workers.

My point is this: members who starve their spouses by ignoring their needs can facilitate their spouses' affairs. Needs may come in the form of conversation, love, laughter, talk, tenderness, touching, physical and emotional intimacy, or a sense of value to another human being. When these needs reach unbearable levels, people can find themselves in behavior that is miles away from their own value system. At this point, their drive to have their needs met is far stronger than their desire to live consistently with their values. Hunger pangs demand relief.

Last night I phoned a politician who my wife and I have known for fifteen years. He was out politicking, so I intended to leave a quick message with his wife and then be on my way. Before hanging up I asked briefly, "By the way, how are you doing, Tracey?" That was all it took. For an hour she affirmed her love for her husband, but admitted she didn't think she could go on much longer. For the past two years, he had spent so much time working on and worrying about his career and finances that he constantly dismissed the depth and legitimacy of her needs. She was crying out for someone to notice, care, and help.

My friend needs to hear what he doesn't want to hear: "If you don't begin to see, hear, and feel your wife's pain, she might find someone else who will. She does not need an impressive politician in her life. She needs a husband, a father, and a live human being who can get into her world. If you keep refusing her request to get into her world, you may be forced to get out of her world. She cannot live with this acute pain and deferred hope much longer."

I find it ironic that some members can spend all their time looking to solve national or world problems while never seeing those in their own marriages and families. Their situations could be illustrated by a forest ranger high up in a look-out tower. The dutiful ranger carefully looks through binoculars across the expansive forest trying to spot forest fires, but while scanning the horizon for smoke, the ranger never notices the fire that's burning in the tower.

Members who are too busy to put the spotlight on their mates should remember Zig Ziglar's response to a question. A man asked him, "When should I tell my wife that I love her?" Ziglar replied, "Before somebody else does."

An empty swimming pool or fuel gauge. Occasionally I ask clients, "Do you think I should stop and buy gasoline for my car on the way home today?" Initially they are perplexed. Their answers are usually something like, "I don't know . . . If you think you need to . . . If you are running low." But I press them gently by saying, "You are telling me to decide by your answer. I am asking you to decide if I should stop and fill my tank." After several rounds of this, the client finally says with some exasperation, "How should I know if you need gas for your car?"

At this moment I get excited and say, "That is exactly right! It is not possible for you to know if I should stop and get gasoline. You have no idea if my tank is three-fourths or one-eighth full. You cannot see my fuel gauge. Only I can see it. That is why it is my primary responsibility to monitor it. No one else can do this for me. I have to know where I am and how much further I can go. Other people cannot detect this for me unless I wait so long that my car begins to sputter, stall, and stop. But by then it is too late."

At this point I explore whether the person I'm interacting with knows how to check their own gauges in life. I am particularly interested in the gauge for their emotional tank. Do they know how to read it? Do they check it regularly? Do they prefer to ignore it? Do they only pay attention to it when it flashes furiously and demands to be noticed? Inattentiveness to one's inner world is a common precursor to an affair. Neglect of one's own needs ultimately makes people desperate for relief.

To make this idea a little clearer, let me ask you to shift word pictures from a fuel gauge to a swimming pool.

Most backyard swimming pools hold about twenty thousand gallons of water. When a pool is full it can handle losing significant amounts of water—loss of one hundred gallons would barely make a difference. But as the pool empties, the less it has to give. It becomes more noticeable each time some water is removed. When the water level reaches the bottom, the removal of any amount is significant. Finally, there is nothing left. No resources remain. There is no reserve.

If you've neglected your inner world you don't need me to tell you the application of this illustration. You know what it is like to be so drained of resources that even the smallest request feels as though it will wipe you out. It is painful, exhausting, overwhelming. You regret ignoring the tell-tale signs—less patience, less tolerance, less joy, less satisfaction, more irritability, depression, and anger.

As the pools of their souls dry up, many try refilling them through affairs. The affairs appear to be the *only* things in their lives that fill the pool rather than drain it. An affair is the only thing that brings pleasure rather than pain. It is the only experience intense enough to remind them that they are alive. A powerful drug, it temporarily numbs their anguish (which they may not even yet recognize) and offers the illusion of joy.

Did You See It Coming?

"Did you see it coming?" It was the same question I ask every person who tells me his spouse has just left him. He simply shook his head and said, "No. I never saw it coming. I thought we had some problems but I never . . ." His response matched 90 percent of those I hear.

How does this happen? How does a person become so spent that he ends up susceptible to finding artificial relief? There are many causes, but let me suggest two that are common on the Hill. One is circumstantial, the other is confusion about self-care.

Cause One: Circumstances. Sometimes circumstances give a person so much to carry that his knees buckle under the weight of the stress. When people don't recognize the enormity of the circumstances they face, they exhaust themselves trying to go about their normal lives. Men, in particular, are very good at ignoring what they are dealing with and its impact on them.

Here are a few circumstances that can drain a person's emotional swimming pool:

financial stress	marital difficulties
work difficulties	health concerns
unresolved grief	parenting struggles
staff problems	campaign difficulties
negative media	inadequate fund-raising
illness	unfinished business

You may be able to come up with additional circumstances which are highly stressful, yet not listed here. It's important that you take inventory of your life and identify those things which may be draining your inner resources, making you more susceptible to having an affair. The real questions are: What specific things have occurred in your life? What is causing you stress? What is the cumulative toll of this stress?

The greater the number, intensity, or duration, the greater the drain on your inner resources. Pay attention.

Cause Two: Confusion about Self-Care. Another common reason for empty emotional tanks is confusion about the differences between self-care, self-abuse, and selfishness.

Some well-meaning individuals do not know how to separate self-care from selfishness. Look at the chart on the next page.

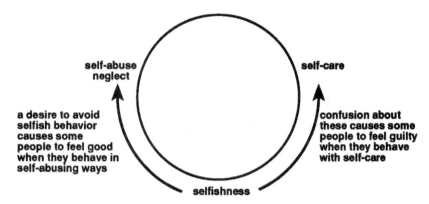

Sometimes when people behave in a manner that is self-caring, they feel selfish and therefore stop the self-caring behavior. They back up so far that they end up neglecting themselves, yet feel good because they no longer feel selfish. Paradoxically, they feel more self-respect when they behave with little self-respect, and they feel disrespect for themselves when they behave in a self-respecting manner. They feel good about themselves when they treat themselves badly, and they feel badly about themselves when they treat themselves well.

A pattern of self-neglect depletes a person's emotional tank.

In some cases, a spouse can reinforce this pattern. Imagine the woman who tells her husband that she is exhausted from taking care of their young children. She wants her husband to give her a needed break. (This request for a break is not necessarily selfish. It may be appropriate self-care.) He replies, "How can you be telling me about this now? Don't you know how much pressure I am under? How can you be so insensitive?"

The inferences from this for the spouse are: 1) Your request is selfish and is not appropriate self-caring; 2) You should feel guilty for being so insensitive to me; and 3) You should return to self-neglect and abuse.

What's really being said is this: "If I can make you feel guilty when you take care of you, then I can continue to expect more of you and give you less. I get to be selfish. I will feel good about it because I will tell you, and myself, that it is really only self-care . . . not selfishness." Savvy linguistic reframing keeps one partner up and the other partner down.

Be warned: Candidates for affairs are not usually men and women on the make. More often than not, they are very ordinary and decent people who were trying to get some needs met—but in an inappropriate manner. Those who live in a chronic state of self-neglect dry out their emotional tank. When this happens, they are vulnerable to having an affair.

If your emotional tank is on empty, you need to keep one other thing in mind: Refilling it is a long process. When a swimming pool holds twenty thousand gallons of water, it takes a long, long time to fill it with a garden hose. If you are close to depletion, a weekend off and a good night of sleep are *not* enough to fill your needs. There is no quick fix.

With the speed of life in Washington, people very easily adopt a lifestyle that is the ideal seedbed for an affair. This is why we need to watch our schedules, avoid starving our mates, and keep our own swimming pools reasonably full.

It is particularly difficult to remember to do these things when we reach mid-life. Affairs cannot be understood without exploring what happens to us during the mid-life years. This is especially true for men. We will look at mid-life for men in the next chapter and then examine techniques to avoid an affair in the chapter that follows.

Think about It

The following questions are for your personal reflection. You may reflect on them alone or discuss them with your spouse, children, or a group of your peers.

1. An affair is defined as an attempt to have legitimate needs met in illegitimate ways. Do you agree with this working definition? Why or why not?

2. Do you agree that the underlying question that leads to most affairs is: How do you spell relief?

3. Is it possible that the schedule and pace of political life could set you or your spouse up for an affair?

4. What needs are most important for you to have met? What needs are most important to your spouse? Are you inadvertently starving each other in any critical areas?

5. Tom suggests that if people get hungry enough they might settle for "junk food" in their relationships. Do you agree or disagree with this?

6. How full is your swimming pool right now? How full is your spouse's? Is each of you aware of how the other is doing or are you simply assuming that you are both all right?

7. There is a distinction made between appropriate self-care, self-abuse, and selfishness. Describe the difference among these three. Where are you most prone to get these confused with each other?

CHAPTER 10

THEY DON'T HAVE TO BE A PACKAGE DEAL

"Do all men become weird in mid-life?"
—Wife of a man in mid-life

Mid-life.[1] It is the only time in a man's life in which he can simultaneously have the vigor and strength of youth and the wisdom of adulthood. It is the one time where physical vitality merges with maturity, wisdom, and insight. Together these can be an awesome combination. Of course, this assumes one is physically in shape and mentally and psychologically mature.

For many men mid-life feels like being stuck in the middle of a long tunnel that has no ends. When some men look back down the tunnel at the last fifteen to twenty years, all they see is hard work, growing responsibility, and diminished pleasure. Then, when they examine their immediate circumstances, they see more of the same: massive amounts of work, responsibility, and pressure.

They feel overwhelmed and sometimes inadequate to manage the numerous responsibilities on their plates. When these men look down the tunnel to their futures, they still see more of the same. There's no end and no exit in sight. They feel trapped inside the stale air of the tunnel.

Entrapment triggers panic in some men. They begin the search for an escape. They need relief . . . anything to avoid feeling inextricably trapped. In desperation, some men make a dumb decision. In order to create a ventilation shaft, they puncture a hole in the tunnel wall. They want to diffuse their pressure, find some relief, obtain some rejuvenation. However, when their self-made ventilation shaft is an affair, it backfires. Instead of releasing the pressure, the self-made shaft can cause the tunnel to collapse in upon itself.

What is it about mid-life that makes men succumb to their circumstances with poor judgment?

When men understand the dynamics of this life stage, they can grow and learn. Indeed, knowledge is power. But lack of understanding can be very destructive—and expensive. Let's look at mid-life and briefly examine a few questions that need to be asked and answered during this time.

Avoiding a Collision

Every day of the work week, thousands of people from Virginia drive into the District of Columbia. To do so, they must cross over the Potomac River. No practical way exists to travel from Virginia to the District without going over one of the bridges. When they do this at rush hour, traffic always backs up on the 14th Street Bridge.

Life is similar to this. No one jumps from youth to maturity without going through mid-life. And, like the 14th Street Bridge, life tends to get very backed up or bogged down during this time. There is a funnel effect. To avoid a collision, this stretch of road has to be carefully navigated.

Recently, I was discussing the mid-life funnel effect with a group of senators. One mentioned that mid-life, like the 14th Street Bridge, is a choke point. It's true. For many men, mid-life is, indeed, a choke point. They choke on the multiple demands pressing for attention in their lives. They choke on their circumstances. They gag on reality—and some men react by spitting it out. Some choke it down. Others chew it and digest it.

In mid-life youth intersects with maturity, fact meets fantasy, and reality encounters myth. A very busy intersection, it is the convergence point for some of the most critical issues we will ever face. During mid-life:

• Youth meets adulthood.

• The reality of what we are meets the expectation of what we thought we would be.

• Physically we begin to "lose our step." We still think fast, but we move a little slower.

• It takes more work to maintain good muscle tone.

• The first hints of memory loss may begin to be evident.

• Some of the old issues, or unfinished business, from our family of origin begin to resurface. Things such as abuse, abandonment, trust, or bonding may need to be faced.

• Time has new value. It begins to be viewed as a limited resource that should be invested wisely.

• The brevity of life is faced, possibly through the death of a parent, sibling, or a close friend.

• The hurts and hungers of the heart are felt more fully.

• The pressures of managing daily life can seem overwhelming. Keeping everyone in the family "clothed and in their right mind" is no easy task.

• Insight and skill are necessary to deal with parents, spouse, children, and self.

When several of these issues swirl in unison, mid-life can be stormy, forcing many men to the brink of their values and the limits of their endurance. But if men use this time for reflection, evaluation, planning, and taking charge of their lives, it can be very positive and helpful in the end. Many come to terms with themselves, their primary relationships, and their work during this time of life. You can, too. If you do the difficult work of assessing where you are, you will be free to make wise calls about where you want to go in the future.

Navigating through the Storm

When the pressure mounts, it's best to stop and evaluate what's going on. Ask yourself what you want to do about the direction in which your life is headed. Will you aggressively play in the game of life or are you going to accept the role of victim? One choice will paralyze you, the other will empower you.

Each man's situation is unique. The following questions were suggested by men who have had the courage to use mid-life as a time of evaluation and planning. They are not comprehensive, but they are all important. Which ones apply to you? It is easy to read these questions quickly. It is not easy to ponder them honestly and then decide what to do with the answers. That is why many men wish they could avoid the analysis that is important in mid-life.

- Do I like who I am and where I am in life right now?

- Do I know and like where I am going?

- Do I feel like a player in the game of life or a victim?

- Do I know the desires and needs of my wife and family?

- Do I care enough about them to remain an actively loving and responsible member of my family?

- Have the multiple responsibilities of our lives pulled my wife and me apart? If so, do I want to deal with this; or, shall I lower my expectations of marriage and say this is all I should expect? Shall I go on doing nothing, drifting further, and hold to the fantasy that this "will straighten itself out in time"?

- Do I make my home a safe and fun place?

- What kind of person am I to come home to? (Some people emanate joy wherever they go. Others have the remarkable ability to eliminate it wherever they go.)

- Do I expect my family to meet all my needs while not being sensitive to theirs?

- Am I holding on to myths or unreal expectations about life and marriage that keep me constantly dissatisfied or angry? (i.e., marriage relationships should always be easy; my spouse should meet all my needs; life should always be easy; healthy relationships do not take work and have no difficulties; if I rid myself of my spouse, most of my problems would disappear.)

- Is it safe for me to speak honestly to my spouse about

things in our marriage that trouble me? Can I risk being honest and open with her?

- Can my wife risk being open and honest with me about things in our marriage that trouble her? Is it safe for her to risk being honest with me?

- Are there legitimate problems or patterns in my marriage that need to be openly discussed because I do not care to live another few decades tolerating things that can and should be changed?

- Do I have values and convictions that are going to guide me through this phase of life or will I simply adjust my values to justify whatever I do?

When counseling men in mid-life, I suggest they ask themselves three additional questions. These questions can help them pinpoint some common mid-life issues.

Have I forgotten to have fun? I've always found it intriguing that grammar school children, who have almost no responsibility, are given time each school day for recess, but adults, who are inundated with personal and professional responsibilities, often assume that they do not need, or cannot afford, moments of play, relaxation, and pleasure.

This may appear noble. But it isn't. People who don't take time out for relaxation and play become candidates for physical or emotional burnout. In time, they may resent their lifestyles. Rather than restoring balance and finding time for appropriately refreshing activities, some have affairs as a covert means of recess in a too-crowded life.

Is my family of origin impacting my relationships as a husband and a father? Many men in mid-life start bouncing off the walls emotionally—and don't know why. They try to ignore what is happening, but they remain confused. If the pain doesn't go away, some men try to externalize the problem and blame it on their spouses, children, or jobs—anything to avoid accepting responsibility themselves.

For some, the struggles and pain from their family of origin resurface. To understand what's going on internally, they will need to explore these old, underlying struggles. Ignoring the root causes of behavior simply prolongs the confusing way these men behave. Often the root causes of mid-life problems revolve around feelings of shame, an inability to form intimate relationships, and issues of power and control.

Shame is one of the most insidious stealers of joy that I observe in my work with people. It robs people of their right to savor and enjoy their accomplishments and success. Some members, despite their extraordinary success, have never been able to drink in the significance and honor of being members of Congress. Instead they live with a secret. They feel thoroughly and profoundly unworthy of being in Congress and fear that their "real person" will be found out by others. They see their lives as charades to be maintained rather than something to be fully enjoyed.

People who live with chronic shame rarely stop to enjoy their accomplishments. The moment they finish something they move on to the next thing because they never find joy or security in what they have just finished. Each accomplishment leaves them with the unconscious conclusion that they are still deeply flawed and unworthy. They will never measure up. Consequently, they focus on the next thing that grabs their attention.

Without knowing why, men who are haunted by shame resent their wives. They feel angry with them. Many want to trade theirs in for a new model—one who is prettier, smarter, sexier.

Look at the picture of the teeter-totter below to understand this subconscious dynamic.

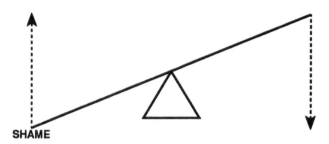

SHAME

Spouse unconsciously expects his/her mate to "lift" them out of shame. Resents or rejects mate when this fails to occur.

The man weighted down by shame keeps unconsciously trying to get unstuck. He wants out of his constant state of feeling inherently inadequate. When he married, he had an expectation neither he nor his wife were aware of: when she sat down on her side of the teeter-totter, she was to lift him out of his shame.

But shame isn't eradicated that way. Over time, and especially in mid-life, many men discover that they are still stuck in their shame. So, without knowing why, they find reasons to reject their spouses. They feel angry and disappointed but are not sure why and cannot articulate their dissatisfaction to their spouses.

What's happening is this: at an unconscious level they are upset that their spouses did not alleviate their pain. Affiliation with their spouses failed to remove their shame. Marriage did not deliver them from their private hell.

But rather than come to grips with their feelings of shame— the root issue of their struggle—many men think it's easier to reject their spouses. That way they can keep the illusion alive that it's possible to find someone who can catapult them out of their shame and into a state of confidence and pride.

Men, no one on the other end of the teeter-totter can lift you out of your shame. A new spouse will not extricate you from the quagmire of your erroneous thoughts and negative emotions. The only way out is to further explore your own beliefs and perceptions about yourself. A skilled counselor can be extremely helpful with this.

Intimacy is another important issue for men in mid-life. Some men wind up in affairs because they hunger to be listened to, taken seriously, and feel respected. When their wives do not have the time, interest, or ability to do this, they may be tempted to seek intimacy elsewhere. But that is not always the case.

Many men are actually terrified of intimacy. Their experiences with their families of origin left them with the belief that intimacy is scary, dangerous, and hurtful. Part of them believes that, "Like gunpowder, if you play with intimacy it will blow up in your face and leave you with powder burns." To help picture this, look at this football field diagram.

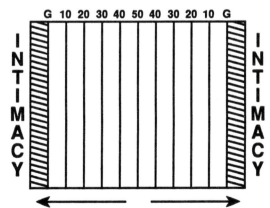

As a couple gets closer to the desired goal of intimacy their unconscious fear of hurt/rejection causes them to find a reason to destroy the intimacy and lower their fear.

Let's assume that a married couple's goal is to reach the end zone where intimacy lies. Ostensibly, at a conscious level, that is the goal they are working toward in their relationship. But, as men get closer to the goal, down at the ten-yard line (inside the red zone where Bear Bryant used to say it is gut check time) a curious thing happens. They fumble the ball or get a penalty. They unconsciously do this to move the ball back toward mid-field. In other words, they do something to destroy the intimacy. They knock the relationship back to mid-field because it feels safer there.

But after they have been safely at mid-field for awhile, they desire more intimacy. So once again, they start marching toward the goal line of intimacy. And, like before, when they get close, they do something to destroy the intimacy and back up the relationship again.

Why do some men do this? Why do they sabotage reaching the goals they desperately want to reach? One reason is a that a conflict exists between their conscious desires and their unconscious expectations.

While genuinely wanting intimacy at one level, many people fear—and expect—rejection and hurt if they risk intimacy. Consequently, as they get closer to intimacy, their unconscious fear takes control. *Once their fear of rejection is stronger than their desire for intimacy, they will do something to sabotage the intimacy.* The goal has shifted from achieving intimacy to avoiding rejection and pain. Once intimacy is destroyed, their fear diminishes. The goal then shifts again and they pursue intimacy . . . until fear starts the cycle all over again.

It's not easy for men to admit they fear intimacy. A couple I knew was stuck in this pattern, but Larry, the husband, could not see it. Every time he and his wife, Brenda, went out on a date and began to connect he would find some reason to destroy the tenderness of the evening.

To expose this pattern I asked Brenda to write down on a three-by-five card, "You will pick a fight with me before we finish our dinner in the restaurant." I asked her to put the card in her purse and bring it out when needed. Right on cue, when the couple began to experience real intimacy, Larry became irritated. As he began to unload on Brenda, she quietly reached into her purse and laid the card on the table for him to read. He was dumbstruck. He finally realized that his problem had little to do with his spouse. It was his struggle. He had to face his fear of intimacy.

Many couples live locked in a pattern of approach-avoidance for years and never know why. Men stuck in this pattern need to look at the root causes of their behavior rather than the surface excuses they find to "pick a fight" and thereby calm their fear of hurt.

Power/control is often the third area of conflict in the marital relationship. The effects of these struggles are easy to spot, but identifying their source is not. It is often tricky. Once again they often go back to the family of origin.

Imagine a husband and wife alone in their home, quarreling. Since no one else is physically present, they assume that they are only arguing with each other. But this isn't really true. This home is actually crowded with other people . . . the significant people of their past. If the force and role of these other individuals is not recognized, couples can get hopelessly confused about what is happening to them, assume that their problems are irreconcilable, and seek a divorce.

Due to this, I often assist clients in identifying "who else is in the room with us?" A person needs to know *who* he is contending with and *why* he is contending with this person, vicariously, through his spouse.

Here is a common example. In mid-life some men begin to feel emotionally harried and disconnected. They desire to have their legitimate needs met. However, if in the backdrop of their lives they have fear or anger about being controlled or dominated, they will be confused about the way they approach meeting their emotional needs.

If a man has been (in reality or perception) dominated by his mother, he may have deep anger and resentment over this experience. Consequently, in his relationship with his wife, he is regularly caught in power struggles that he does not understand. He reacts strongly to his wife because she now has the misfortune of identification with the man's mother with whom he is still angry.

In order for a man like this to have intimacy, he must first establish control. *After* he has done this, he feels safe enough to approach his wife looking for physical and emotional intimacy. But he will enjoy it only as long as his wife appears weak, hurt, and non-threatening.

The pattern looks like this. A man picks a fight with his wife. He unconsciously wants to hurt her because when she is wounded and in pain he feels safe. How can a broken and wounded person hurt, dominate, or threaten him? So, now that he has wounded his wife, he feels secure enough to approach her for physical and emotional intimacy. It is an unconscious pattern that says, "I have to hurt you before I can freely love you and let you love me."

This strange logic is far more common than people think. Occasionally men (and women, too) become so confused by this pattern that they assume marriage cannot ever work smoothly. So they check out or have an affair. In the process, they never come face-to-face with the core issues.

If you are feeling dissatisfied with your marriage and your spouse, I cannot stress enough how important it is that you honestly evaluate whether you struggle with shame, intimacy, or power/control.

Do I want to grow up? Initially, this may seem like a foolish question to be asking a grown man. But many men, like Peter Pan, don't want to grow up. First Corinthians 13, the well-known chapter on love, addresses this issue: "When I was a child, I spoke like a child, I thought like child, I reasoned like a child; when I became a man, I gave up childish ways."

If we are to enjoy healthy adult relationships as men, we must give up childish ways. Thinking selfishly and irresponsibly is okay for very young children—but not for adults.

Do you want to grow up?

This is not an easy question. It is one of the major decisions of mid-life. At the gut level, many men would like to cry out, "No. I don't want to grow up. I want my life to be consistently fun and easy. I want pleasure, not pressure. I want people to care about me and cater to me. I want people to make me the center of their worlds the way they did when I was a child. I want all the privileges of adulthood with the minimal responsibilities of a youth. I want the right to play and never grow up. I want to stay in never-never land. And, I will resent anything or anyone that interferes with this desire."

Mid-life will indeed interfere with this wishful fantasy. It loads men up with multiple responsibilities. They have professional, social, civic, financial, marital, and parental responsibilities that are not going to disappear. Men need to decide how they will respond to the realities of mid-life. They have essentially three options: running, resenting, or resolving.

Some men simply run. They want to escape their primary responsibilities and relationships. They try to chase the illusion that life can forever be simple, carefree, and without difficulty.

Other men decide to remain in their primary relationships, but they don't attempt to face or resolve the normal issues that arise during mid-life. As a result, they often become quietly frustrated and resentful of feeling trapped. Even though they have chosen to stay in their marriages, they are unhappy and at a loss for knowing how to make their marriages more satisfying and fulfilling. These men then separate or compartmentalize their lives. They want to do the right thing, so they choose to fulfill their responsibilities to their wives and families. But they do not expect these relationships to fulfill their needs for pleasure, release, or attention. So they develop a separate means of meeting these needs via an affair.

Lastly, some men choose to hit mid-life head-on. They resolve the issues of mid-life. They do not deny the power, legitimacy, or usefulness of all that is occurring during this stage of life. They embrace these things and wrestle with them. In doing so, they learn, grow, change, and mature. They usually emerge from this stretch of life more content with themselves, their marriages, and their families. They end up the winners.

If you want to reach maturity, you must cross the bridge of mid-life. But you don't need to dread reaching the 14th Street Bridge of mid-life. It can be one of the most dynamic and life-changing phases of your life.

You can navigate this stretch of road wisely and avoid doing something dumb. The choice is up to you. But remember, the consequences of your choice will ripple down into the next several generations.

Funny thing about life—we can control our choices, but not the consequences of those choices. To ensure that we make wise choices, it helps to know how to identify the early stages of an affair. If you realize that you are a candidate for an affair, you can predetermine what your choice will be. That's the topic of the next chapter.

Note

1. In this chapter I am viewing mid-life from a man's point of view. To go beyond that is outside my experience and research. My queries on this subject have come from very careful and extended interviews with male members.

Think about It

The following questions are for your personal reflection. You may reflect on them alone or discuss them with your spouse, children, or a group of your peers.

1. Mid-life is presented as having the potential of being positive and life-changing. Do you agree with this?

2. Mid-life is also presented, for some men, as analogous to being stuck in the middle of a long tunnel that has no ends in sight. Do you agree with this?

3. What important things are in the tunnel of your life at this moment? How are these things influencing you?

4. What questions or issues are you wrestling with at this moment?

5. Have you and your family remembered how to have fun? What has your family done recently that gave you all a heart of laughter and a memory for a lifetime?

6. Is the concept of shame new to you? Is it something that you think might be playing a significant role in your life?

7. Is attaining and/or avoiding intimacy a struggle in your life? Is it an issue in your spouse's life?

8. Do you agree that mid-life forces people to answer the question, "Do you want to grow up?" How would you answer this question?

CHAPTER 11

RESISTING AN AFFAIR

"Either you will make up your mind about an affair,
or your unmade mind will unmake you."
—Jay Allen Petersen

We were meeting in the senator's hideaway office. Like all hideaways, it was located in a remote part of the Capitol where the public rarely goes. I arrived early, so I found a chair in the hall and waited. To kill some time, I decided to review some notes on people involved in affairs.

As I was looking at the material, an older senator quietly slipped out of his hideaway, combing his hair and straightening his suit as he walked down the hall. I thought to myself, "These remote offices would be the ultimate meeting place for a member to have an affair." Five minutes later, out of the same office, came a beautiful woman who was easily twenty years younger than the senator. As I watched her walk away, I mused, "Yeah, right, tending to the nation's business." My assumptions about what they were up to could have been wrong . . . but I don't think so.

While I sat there, I wondered how these two people, and so many others like them, became enmeshed in an affair. I wondered if they knew how to see one developing and how to avoid it. Many adults, especially those in the work force, will be confronted with the opportunity for an affair. It is a wise man or woman who has done some contingency planning on his or her response to this moment. How does an individual skillfully avoid the seductive lure of an affair? With a game plan, it can easily be done. Without a game plan, people can easily be done in.

Have you seen Michael Jackson do the "moonwalk"? It is a dance step which looks like he is walking forward while in reality he is moving backward. The early stages of an affair are often like that. People convince themselves and others that they are going in one direction when they are really headed in the exact opposite direction.

There is a gentle, slow seduction in most relationships that end in an affair. They develop subtly and covertly. Often, in the very beginning, neither party initially knows what he or she is doing or experiencing. Later, when they become aware of it, they tell themselves that they really are not doing anything inappropriate, unprofessional, or illegitimate. They utilize denial and rationalization very effectively at this point.

If the two individuals keep "playing with their relationship," it may become apparent to other colleagues that something is happening. They may not be certain, but they have a hunch. Usually, the parties involved, if asked, would vehemently deny any entanglement. They would accuse the observers of misunderstanding their friendship, their need to spend time together for work related reasons, etc.

When they eventually do admit to themselves what they are doing and playing with, they often think they can keep it under control. They still are not doing anything overtly wrong. It could be that neither individual has openly acknowledged their attraction to the other. They are simply enjoying how easily they relate to one another. This leaves them in a world of curiosity and fantasy, wrapped in the cover of innocence and denial. They rationalize that they are only dealing with their thoughts . . . nothing more.

Such a slippery slope could easily become an avalanche. It could easily become a full-blown affair. Sadly, many people never acknowledge this until it is too late. Either they are unwilling or incapable of detecting the indicators of an affair in the making.

Early Warning Signs

If you want to be able to head off an affair at its early stages, you must have:

1. The ability to *recognize* the early warning signals.

2. The ability to *avoid denial* when the early warning signals are evident.

Early detection. For people with cancer or heart problems, early diagnosis often spells the difference between treatable and terminal. If corporations don't anticipate changes in the market, economy, or their cash flow, they are dead. And, in the political world, when politicians don't accurately detect changes in their constituency or the political climate, they can be changed from a lawmaker to a lobbyist on the first Tuesday in November.

The same is true for affairs: the sooner they are identified, the easier they are to manage. But, like most things that are frightening, it is easy to ignore the early indicators.

As we noted earlier, in the embryonic stages of an affair, most people play fast and loose with the facts. They know they have more than just a casual interest in this individual, but they manage the interest with massive doses of rationalization and denial. This neutralizes their internal conflicts and fears for a time. It blurs reality and enables them to keep "innocently toying" with the relationships.

When I counsel someone who I believe is on the brink of an affair, I ask, "Do you think you are headed toward an affair, or possibly already in one?" Many people (especially males) will insist that the answer is no. However, when our work is complete and they are asked to look back and see if the early warning signs were evident, and if they knew it at the time, they invariably answer, "Yes. I knew what I was doing. At some level I was aware of what was going on. I was just not willing to admit it to myself because I did not want to stop."

As a counselor, it is imperative that I know how to detect the early signs of inappropriate attraction to a woman. To say I am not attracted to someone on occasion would make me a liar. To ignore the signs would make me a fool.

Counselors have the advantage of having clear, firm boundaries on the purpose, format, place, time, and frequency of being with others. In my counseling practice I generally see people once a week for fifty minutes. Those minutes are spent in a one-sided relationship where we focus only on my client's life issues, not my life or needs.

But most people spend many hours a week together in settings with much fuzzier boundaries. They may spend the entire workday in the same office, attend the same meetings, go to lunch, or travel together. There is a much greater likelihood of people in these settings becoming emotionally or physically involved in a two-way relationship. For them the distinction between being professional, professionally friendly, friendly, or personal is much more blurred. That is why all adults can benefit from the ability to recognize the early indicators of attraction to another individual.

Below are some of the warning signs that have to be recognized and taken seriously if someone wants to avoid "moonwalking" into an affair.

- Are you looking forward to being with this person?
- Are you thinking or wondering about the person at random moments in the day?
- Are you willing to give her extra time, or more time than you would give to others?
- Are you willing to give her extra assistance and finding that you are enjoying it rather than feeling interrupted?
- Are you noting what you will wear when you are going to be with this person?
- Are you more animated or energetic when you are with her?
- Are you more willing to give her your undivided attention?
- Are you happy to listen more carefully to her?
- Is your posture better when you are with this person? Are you trying to look your best?
- Do you smile more when you are with her?
- Do you look more directly into her eyes?
- Are you "talking more" with your eyes? Are they open

wider and more animated? Have you noticed that your eyebrows are moving more as you speak with this person?

- Are you willing to be physically closer to her than you normally are with others? Are you looking for ostensibly legitimate reasons to be very near her?

- When you join a group do you first look to see if she is there? Are you excited if she is and disappointed if she is not?

- If she is in a group, do you try to find at least a brief moment to be together?

- Do you secretly resent others in the group because they are preventing you from talking to or being with this person?

- Are you more willing or eager to touch this person? (Whether via comforting her, teasing her, brushing near her, or handing her some paper doesn't matter. The issue is, are you looking for little ways to make brief contact that seems innocuous.)

- Are your topics of conversation with this person beginning to be more personal and intimate?

If you can answer several of these questions in the affirmative, there is reason for you to be cautious and careful in your interaction and time with the individual on your mind. I recommend you take the zoo keeper's advice: *Don't feed the tigers.* Tigers in the zoo may look beautiful, serene, and docile and give the impression of being safe, manageable, and approachable. But tigers are also swift and too strong to be wrestled with successfully. The same is true for the passion and lust of an affair. It's best not to feed the tiger in the first place—that way it can't overpower you when you least expect it.

A Game Plan

Most people have no familiarity with the early warning signals of a potential affair—and most have no game plan for what to do if they find themselves being drawn into an affair. Let me suggest a game plan I learned from an old politician who was trying to teach his children about the power of lust and the lure of adultery: King Solomon. You can find his advice in the seventh chapter of Proverbs.

Solomon paid dearly for his wisdom in this area. Like so many people in our culture today, he had a struggle with impulse control that he refused to deal with until enormous damage had been done. But I am always glad to obtain wisdom from someone else's mistakes rather than making more of my own.

If you read Solomon's honest and loving counsel to his children, you will notice that he explained the dynamics of adultery. He articulates how lust is fed, how affairs begin, and how they often end.

As a game plan Solomon recommends three simple things to keep in mind to avoid getting caught in an affair.

1. Watch the settings you are in. Being cautious about the settings you allow yourself to be in may seem simplistic, impossible, or just old-fashioned. In reality, it is one of the most simple and sure safeguards people can employ against behavior that violates their value systems. Paying attention here can save a lifetime of regrets later. Clear standards have a way of protecting people from unnecessary scar tissue in life.

People need to decide ahead of time what safeguards are

appropriate and manageable for them. I generally don't worry about those whose standards are too high . . . but I do fear for those who have few or no guidelines in this area.

Here are some of the standards that members have utilized to protect themselves from settings that could compromise their character or conduct. These members are:

- Not willing to travel alone (by car or plane) with a colleague of the opposite sex.

- Not willing to work late at night with only one other colleague of the opposite sex.

- Not willing to have adjoining hotel rooms with colleagues of the opposite sex

- Not willing to go out after work for dinner or drinks with anyone of the opposite sex.

- Not willing to meet someone of the opposite sex in their office unless the door is open or another person sits in on the meeting.

These guidelines, and others like them, are not always easy or practical. Nor are they always understood or respected by others. But individuals who have some non-negotiable standards in this area are protecting themselves against moments of vulnerability. In moments of weakness, people need their environment to work for them, not against them. A setting that encourages right choices rather than poor ones is a great asset in some of life's critical moments.

Numerous members and staffers have been caught off guard by an absence of some simple, firm guidelines that they live by. I have repeatedly seen people on the Hill who got caught in the late-night hours of Hill-related work.

It goes like this. The member and some of his or her staff have been working long and hard on some endeavor such as a major campaign event. Planning this event takes enormous amounts of time, attention, and emotional energy. As they work together on the project, several things occur simultaneously.

They feel like a team from working so hard and focusing together on the event. An *esprit de corps* develops. They sense that they are in something together and standing side by side. They develop an "us against them" mentality. They are partners, colleagues, "one."

Meanwhile the member's marital relationship back home is sagging. His personal life and needs are neglected. His emotional tank is low, and he is feeling out of sync with his spouse. He is out of touch with his spouse's world and feels that his spouse is out of touch with his world.

It occurs to him that his work colleague understands and cares more about the all-consuming event than his spouse does. From here, it is a small step (although an erroneous one) to conclude that "my colleague understands my life, my pressures, my needs, and my priorities more than my mate does." This moment makes it easy for the member to resent his mate and more ready to respond to the colleague.

With these dynamics in place it is dangerous for members not to guard their work settings. Their emotional needs are up and their fatigue is high. Their marital satisfaction is low and their resistance is down. Their perceptions are skewed. When this combination is mixed with long, late-night hours alone with a colleague, the setting can become a perfect set up for an affair. All it takes is one moment where one of them briefly drops their guard and moves from the professional to the personal. In that instant, provided by a setting that afforded them no restraint, they can learn one of life's most difficult lessons: *Unguarded moments can yield uncommon responses.* They can swiftly find themselves doing and saying things with that colleague that they never thought possible.

I know this pattern. Because, when their head clears, they often call and ask me to help them understand what happened. "One thing lead to another and before we knew it . . ." I have heard it often enough that I unashamedly tell people to pay very close attention to the settings and situations they allow themselves to be in with colleagues of the opposite sex.

2. Watch your speech. This is another practice that allows people to protect themselves from compromising circumstances. Like watching the settings in which we allow ourselves to be, this may seem simplistic. It is not. It is another safeguard.

I am fascinated by the power of language and words. People's lives are often profoundly shaped by a few words from some significant person in their lives. The words can be positive or negative, but either way the impact may last a lifetime. To test this, all you have to do is pause and recall the nicknames that your family or friends had for you when you were a child. The names are quickly recalled and they can still carry a great deal of emotional weight.

While people recognize the power of words in general, they often overlook the force of language in their conversations with others. Some may *know* the force of language but they want to play with it anyway. They engage in linguistic Russian roulette. They use loaded language in their conversations with others while acting as if they have done nothing at all.

Office language is often full of double entendre or double

speak. The language has an acceptable surface content that makes it seem legitimate. But underneath, there is a layer of intent or meaning that is loaded with innuendoes. The underlying message may be angry, hostile, tender, or sexual. Many people in affairs look back and see that they were involved in sexual or very personal dialogue masked in daily conversation long before their emotions were openly acknowledged.

Words reflect our thoughts and emotions. They represent what already lies within us. But words and conversation also have the power to create new thoughts, emotions, and behaviors. While this is a great asset in normal life, it can be dangerous if it is used casually. Most people are seduced by language long before they physically capitulate to an affair.

People who are careful to guard their speech and their settings rarely stumble into an affair. They are seldom caught in that weak moment where, as Solomon puts it, "all at once he goes, as an ox goes to the slaughter." They do not find themselves in the position of acting impetuously because they are willfully guarding their environments and emotions, rather than being controlled by them.

Those who choose to ignore these precautions often learn a difficult lesson: Inappropriate attraction to another individual is best managed in its early stages and should be treated with respect and caution.

"My Advice to You Is . . ."

As I've worked with members who have struggled to protect their marriages and themselves in this area, I've come up with these additional guidelines. They are boundaries that members have established to ensure that they win in the game of life.

1. Put on your jogging shoes when you are attracted to an affair. Those readers who know me know that I am not a timid or passive guy. I am a firm proponent of people being strong and courageous and holding their ground when it is appropriate. However, when it comes to the seductive power of an affair, I change my posture dramatically. I encourage people to run. Actively avoid the opportunity. It is not macho to try to manage this struggle. It is foolish. I would rather look like a wimp who ran away and won at the game of life, than some fool whose life blew up because he toyed with something he naively assumed he could handle.

2. In moments of temptation live by your convictions, not by your emotions. When pilots get vertigo, they learn to trust their guidance system and ignore their instincts—even when their instincts insist they are right. People in affairs almost always suffer from vertigo, and they need more than their own perceptions to guide them. Don't let your emotions guide you in moments of temptation. If you do, buckle your seat belt and be sure that your insurance is paid. You are likely to crash.

3. Stay rooted in reality. An enormous distortion results when an individual compares a relatively unknown third party to his spouse. He usually compares his brief moments with an idealized person to multiple years with a spouse, who also may not be seen with any reality. The spouse is viewed negatively and the third party is viewed positively. One can do no right. The other can do no wrong. Both views are distorted.

4. Remember that it is a privilege to have a life partner. If you have lost your appreciation and love for your spouse, invest the time and energy to discover what is happening. Resolve your struggles. Don't run from them or act them out.

It is an enormous privilege to face life's adventures with someone who is committed to you as a life companion. And, as we get older, there will come a time when we will enjoy looking back as much as we savor looking ahead.

When I reminisce on the landmark moments of my life and family, I want to do it with someone who was right there with me. I want to be with the person who was there when our children arrived and when our parents exited. I want to be with someone who remembers when we had little maturity, massive naiveté, and no money . . . but were as happy as ever. I want to be with someone who remembers the grind of graduate schools and the joy of advanced degrees granted. I want to be with someone who recalls the confusion of parenting and the happy surprise at the results. I want to be with someone who understands a man who "stumbled" onto Capitol Hill and found a group of people he loves and cares about. I want to be with someone who saw my struggles, defeats, and victories. I want to be with someone who saw me play the game of life and knows the meaning of it for me because she was there. And I want to do the same thing for her.

I believe having a marriage partner is a priceless asset. We need to be wise enough to treasure it in "the here and now." If we don't, it may not be there in the "then and there."

5. *Remember the consequences of an affair.* Affairs are not inexpensive. They destroy trust, ruin reputations, and cause a part of you to die.

Some years ago I was consulting with Dr. Bill Secor, a psychologist who has been both a mentor and a friend to me. He mentioned a client who had always believed that if he had an affair he would die. The client finally had one and defiantly said, "And I did not die."

But he was wrong. He did die. He died in multiple ways. His ability to face himself with a pure heart and a clear conscience died. His ability to face his wife and children with freedom and integrity died. His ability to be open with his closest friends died. And his ability to face his Creator with confidence died. He died psychologically, emotionally, maritally, socially, and spiritually. His affair may have been fun for the moment, but at great cost.

6. *If you want to flirt, go ahead and do it—with your spouse.* If people would put the same level of eagerness, energy, attentiveness, cheerfulness, and flexibility into their marriages that they put into some third party who intrigues them, their marriages would flourish rather than languish. When marriages are fulfilling and healthy, an affair seems ridiculous to even consider.

7. *Watch out for star seekers.* Because of your position as a member of Congress, you are—in a tragic sense—a big prize for some people. Many opportunists would enjoy romantic involvement with a member. They want to be associated with "a star." That is why, as one Congressional wife told me, members need to be careful of the star seekers.

Members need to establish clear boundaries regarding their beliefs and behaviors *before* they are confronted with the option of an affair. Having a clear game plan makes it much easier to resist the lure of an affair.

I don't know how the senator whom I saw emerge from his hideaway began his relationship with the woman who followed him. But if he or the woman had a game plan that was instantly implemented at the moment of intrigue, they never would have ended up alone. Most people I meet who have been involved in an affair, never wanted or intended to be in one. They backed into one because they did not see or admit what was happening. They had no game plan. Even with a healthy marriage, a game plan for avoiding an affair is invaluable. The proverbial "ounce of prevention" protects the unsuspecting from getting mauled by a tiger they thought was safe. The next chapter covers one more way to "affair-proof" your marriage.

Think about It

The following questions are for your personal reflection. You may reflect on them alone or discuss them with your spouse, children, or a group of your peers.

1. It is suggested there is a "gentle, slow, seduction in most relationships that end up in an affair." Do you agree or disagree with this?

2. How do you distinguish between relationships that are professional, professionally friendly, friendly, or personal?

3. Look at the list of "warning signs to watch." Which ones make the most sense to you? Which ones are the greatest indicator to you that you need to be cautious? Can you think of other warning signs?

4. What boundaries or guidelines have you set for yourself that might be helpful to others? Do you think it is wise or naive to have professional boundaries in dealing with people?

5. Should you ever find yourself intrigued with the "option of an affair," what is your game plan?

CHAPTER 12

SAFE HARBORS

"He who walks with wise men becomes wise."

Since I was a young boy I wanted to be a congressman more than anything in the world." The member's voice reflected his pain. "It was my life's dream and I achieved it ten years ago. When I arrived here my son was seven years old. I was too busy to have much to do with him. Now he is seventeen and he doesn't want anything to do with me. First I broke his heart, and now he is breaking mine. We are this far apart." As he said this, he stretched his arms. "And do you know what? I would give all of this up . . . just to have a relationship with my son."

This member's story reminds me of a comment I once heard from an astute elderly person. Reflecting on her life she smiled and said, "Too soon old and too late wise."

How could this member have been wise while his son was still young and eager for his father's love, time, guidance, and approval? What could have helped him make better judgment calls during his early years in Congress? What might help him now in dealing with the loss and pain? Where can he get insight in attempting to restore his relationship with his son and the rest of his family? Where can he, and others like him, discover how to balance home life while serving in Congress?

A significant part of the answer to these questions lies in members finding a safe harbor, a harbor of friendships where they can safely speak about the storms of life that they are weathering. It is what I call "interior friendships." A group of people with whom it is safe for you to be candid.

You can let these people into the interior portions of your life. They will not be shocked when you inform them that you wrestle with exactly the same things that all of us mortals struggle with in life. These people allow you the freedom to acknowledge your humanness while laying down your image of having it all together. They give you permission to be real. Human. Normal. It is a wonderful gift.

Safe harbors and interior friendships provide an environmentally safe place to talk over the issues written about in this book. Sometimes, while discussing these issues, people happily discover that they are managing numerous areas of life very well and they can be available to listen and consider giving perspective to someone else. Other times, as they discuss life in Congress, they realize they need to make some changes before it's too late.

Some readers probably can't imagine making time to talk openly with a few trusted friends. It is the antithesis of how they have lived much of their lives. They are more accustomed to stuffing their struggles, hiding their hurts, and staying so busy that they don't have time to be in touch with what, and how, they are doing. They try to sustain an image and manage a career. Anything outside of this paradigm seems impertinent, uncomfortable, and a waste of time.

Political life also feeds this habit of maintaining an upbeat and positive front. Members are afraid they will appear politically vulnerable if it becomes known that they have any problems in their lives, so they try to conceal or minimize any physical problems or other personal struggles. They don't want the truth about them to be known by many people due to the ever-present fear that it will jeopardize their careers. Consequently, their lives often become very isolated. Very private. Profoundly alone. Fortunately (and unfortunately) their full schedules usually keep them from facing the emptiness of their lives.

Many members have never been involved in meeting weekly with a group of friends to keep balance in their lives. So when they are invited to attend such a meeting they are understandably curious. They ask the inevitable question: Who else participates? But they are even more curious about what goes on in the group. They want to know: What do you do? How is the time spent? Why is it meaningful for the participants?

They also wonder if they will be asked to discuss things that are too personal for them. (This does not happen. Ever.) They wonder, as I once did, if people who meet weekly in groups are weak or weird. I discovered years ago that people who make time to participate in small groups are some of the most balanced, growing, and secure people I know. I now worry more about those individuals who have no safe harbors or interior friendships. Life was never intended to be a solo act.

So, what's a small group like?

How Do You Set Up a Small Group?

The format of small groups I've been involved with is quite simple. We meet once a week for one hour. We spend the first ten to fifteen minutes just relaxing and catching up with one another. After this we usually look at a passage of Scripture to use as a text for our topic and discussion. Our goal is to see how the text pertains in practical ways to our immediate lives. (While I have a doctorate in psychology, with a specialty in family psychology, I have enormous respect for the psychological health that can result from taking the spiritual aspect of life seriously.) Then, at the end of the hour, we take a few moments for closing prayer.

What happens during our time is life-changing.

Most of us in the group have been running at full tilt all day before entering the room so the first part of the meeting is important for stress management. Members finally have an opportunity simply to slow down and rest. They get a brief respite from the relentless rush of their daily lives. It is both welcome and needed.

In the early moments of our time, members do a lot of "small talk." There is often a lot of kidding and laughing. But this too is enormously important because healthy and appropriate laughter is one of the most delightful and refreshing gifts of life. It is energizing and stress-reducing. Additionally, in taking time for small talk people get to know each other as individuals. It's a springboard for future friendship.

As we discuss the Scriptural passage, we gain perspective

about life in the bigger picture. This perspective comes from various sources. Much of it comes from members talking with each other about how they handle different aspects of life. In doing this they become models and mentors for one another. And the collective wisdom of these prodigiously gifted people is quite impressive. (So is the depth of their character and the sincerity with which they approach their work.) Their practical insights can be extremely timely and helpful.

The Scriptures are another source of practical wisdom that lend perspective to the participants. While clearly affirming the dignity and worth of the individual, they also help us to see beyond ourselves to life as a whole. This larger view of life is essential if we are to live with sensitivity to those around us. The Scriptures help us keep the very thing that is so easy to lose in public life: balance in our personal lives.

At the end of our time together, most of us walk out the door and resume the frantic pace of our daily lives—but we have just experienced something unique. We have just spent an hour that was relaxing, refreshing, and relevant. Why? Because in that brief time we had the freedom to be real and get reconnected with life. We had the opportunity to feel respected, cared for, and taken seriously. And we did this same thing for others.

We got in touch with ourselves, our colleagues, our Creator, and our lives. We remembered that we are not alone; that wisdom and encouragement can be found through friends and the scriptures; and that balance, perspective, and peace can be augmented when we invest time in a safe harbor.

I have heard numerous members say during a group discussion:

"This is the most meaningful hour of my week."

"This is the only place where I have seen members be real with each other about their lives."

"This is one of the few places where members are honestly attempting to know one another and build friendships."

"This is one of the few places where members meet in a nonpartisan setting. Like cowboys in the old west that had to check their six-shooters at the door before entering a saloon, we check our politics at the door before entering. It is very refreshing."

"This is the only hour of my week that is designed to rejuvenate me rather than to extract something from me."

"When I leave Congress this is the only group of members that I will miss. And it is probably the only group that will miss me."

One day one of my dearest friends in Congress, a liberal, started laughing and spontaneously told a conservative in the group, "You know, I have to tell you something. I used to think you were a kook. A complete wacko. Now that I've gotten to know you I have discovered that you are a very nice guy and also very bright. I really like you."

Gary, a member who has just begun dropping in on one of the small groups told me, "I don't mean to hurt your feelings, Tom. But I don't come to the group to hear you teach or for the discussions. I come because this is the first place I have seen since becoming a congressman where I can develop friendships with other members." What he lacked in diplomacy, he made up for in sincerity. I told him I was glad for his comments and his participation in the group.

I wish the congressman who stopped me in the Capitol to tell me about his estranged relationship with his son had participated in a weekly discussion group since his arrival in Washington. One cannot know for sure, but there is a good chance it would have helped him keep the whole of his life in balance and in perspective. But, like so many others, he was duped by the Washington mystique. He thought his work was too important and his schedule too full to make a safe harbor of friendships. Like the rest of us, he cannot undo the events of his life. But if he wants to find a place of insight and concern for his present and future life, he would serve himself by making time to meet with a group of peers who have made it a priority to think about what matters most in life.

Think about It

The following questions are for your personal reflection. You may reflect on them alone or discuss them with your spouse, children, or a group of your peers.

1. Have you made it a priority to maintain balance in your personal life? Or is this something you talk about doing sometime in the indefinite future?

2. This week, when I finished writing this chapter, I heard of a freshman member not running for re-election because his children needed more time with him. He said, "It is not possible to be a good dad and a congressman at the same time." What do you think about his comments and his decision?

3. Where do you go, or what do you do, to keep yourself tethered to reality while serving in public office?

4. How do you protect regular time for yourself and your primary relationships?

5. Safe harbors are described as a place where friends can talk with a degree of openness about their lives. Do you have a group like this that you meet with on a regular basis?

6. What is the most meaningful hour of your week?

7. Do you have any interior friendships in Congress? Who are they? Have you thanked them for the meaningful role they play in your life?

8. Do you meet with anyone who is keeping you balanced as a whole person—physically, emotionally, socially, and spiritually?

9. Do you have some false assumptions, as Tom did, about the benefit of meeting in a weekly group with peers?

CHAPTER 13

POSTSCRIPT FOR SPIN CONTROL

ajor political speeches given at national political conventions
intrigue me. I enjoy watching who speaks, what they say, and
how they say it. However, one aspect of the media coverage
invariably irritates me. I find it both insulting and demeaning. It occurs immediately after the speech when the media ana-
lysts come on to tell the audience what they just heard in the
speech. I wonder if they think we did not hear what was said
because of audio difficulty with our television or do they think
their audience is too dumb to comprehend what they just listened
to? I need them to provide coverage of these events. But I do not
need them to be or provide spin doctors for me.

Knowing this is a part of Washington life, I want to do some spin control myself regarding this book. Let me clarify once again the motivation and intent of this work. This book is written for individuals serving in Congress. I care deeply about them. Their families and individual well-being matter to me. My hope is that this text will be received as a helpful tool for them. My goal is that it provides practical insight about something members rarely have time to think about—their personal lives.

It is also an initial response to a question I have asked scores of members, "What book has been most helpful in preparing you to understand how political life can impact your personal life?" Almost without exception, they answer that they have never read, nor heard of such a book. One member lamented, "Many people want to write *about us,* Tom, but no one wants to write *for us.* "

I've tried to walk a line that is honest and insightful while still being sensitive and fair. I have attempted to write frankly about some of the struggles that I have seen repeatedly in my time on the Hill. Without honesty and candor a friend cannot be helpful to others. But I do not mean to write disparagingly of those who serve in Congress. Already too much ruthless exploration by the media of politicians' personal lives occurs.

I have enormous regard for the majority of those who serve in the Legislative Branch. I am not disenchanted with them as many people currently are. Members are no different than any other large group of people that one would get to know well. A few are flakes, phonies, or showboats. Some should retire. And a handful are public relations experts that in reality do little work and have minimal substance.

I am convinced, though, that the bulk of the Congress con-sists of people who have a deep love and concern for our country.

They are people who genuinely care about their constituents and find enormous satisfaction in helping others. They are exceptionally hard workers who cope with pressures that would make most people snap. And they are people who approach their work with high integrity and an honest belief that what they are doing is best for America. I am glad to call many of them my friends.

Let me say thank you to the many members and their families who have trusted me with the stories and emotion of their political and private lives. I have been honored by your trust, and I hope you do not feel it has been abused in any way. I think you know me well enough to know I have attempted to write with care and in a spirit of love. Those of you who know me best know two things: I want you to win where it matters most, and, I am in your corner. May our co-laboring on this book be a help to you and your present and future colleagues.

APPENDIX

A QUICK REVIEW

Following is a quick review of some of the topics proposed in this book as common areas of concern for members who want to succeed in their private lives while serving in public office. You might find it helpful to periodically review these points to be sure that you are managing your life effectively.

- Remember to get out of the spotlight and focus it on others—especially your family.

- It is okay for you to want your family to get into your mud puddle. But you also need to get into their mud puddles as well.

- Even though members live incredibly busy and pressured lives, we cannot ask our families to hold their breath longer than is feasible. Are there signs of oxygen deprivation in your home?

- Be careful not to expect your family to agree to the "unwritten contract" where the fine print suggests that they accommodate your needs and career as they accept the fact that you will not be able to accommodate them because your job is so consuming.

- Avoid asking your spouse to run hidden marathons in the back alleys of life with little support from you and others, while expecting her to be sensitive to the difficulty of your race in the public arena.

- Remember: Quality friendships are a result of investing time and risking trust, and a willingness to initiate disclosure. Life in Congress can make one so guarded that the capacity for these is diminished rather than developed.

- It is easy to confuse having fans with having friends. They are not the same thing. But, for some members, a crowd is as good as a friend.

- Sometimes it seems easier to marry our work than to work at our marriage. Some days the "bubble" of Capitol Hill is much more tolerable than the reality of home life.

- Our schedules need to be managed if we are serious about managing our lives. Life as a member exerts enormous pressure on values and can throw schedules completely out of line with priorities.

- Sufficient hunger can make anyone a candidate for an affair. The speed and distortion of Congressional life can first create the problem of hunger and then provide the solution via an affair.

- Mid-life. It is an important and dynamic phase of life. But for some men it feels like being stuck in the middle of a long tunnel. Feeling trapped and needing fresh air, many of them create a ventilation shaft through an affair. It is a dubious means of relief and refreshment.

- Mid-life confronts men with significant questions about who they are, where they are in life, and what they want out of life. Some men tackle the questions and others simply deny or run from them.

- The ability to discuss these topics, and others, with colleagues who understand is very freeing. When colleagues take time to think and talk honestly about life (including their own), perspective and balance can be maintained or restored.

To order more copies of this book and for more information about speaking engagements, corporate consulting, or counseling, write or call:

Dr. Tom Barrett
Business/Life Management, Inc.
1980 Gallows Road, Suite 200
Vienna, Virginia 22182

Voice mail: (703) 247-4314
Fax: (703) 356-3485

For your convenience use the coupon below to order more books:

✂--

Mail to: Business/Life Management, Inc.
          1980 Gallows Rd., Suite 200
          Vienna, VA 22182

My check or money order for $17.95 per book is enclosed. (Please make checks payable to B.L.M., Inc. and include an additional $1.50 for each book ordered to cover shipping and handling.)

Please charge my Visa/Master Card Acct# _____
Exp. Date _____

Name _____

Address _____

City _____ State/Zip _____

Telephone No. _____

* Quantity discounts available upon request